612/
(500)

604

J11604

Everyday Science written by: Michael Gabb
Illustrated by: Derek Bunce, Roger Full Associates, John Harwood,
John Kelly, Jack Pelling, Mike Roffe, Mike Saunders,
Tony Simmonds, David Worth
Cover illustrated by: Alun Hood

The Body Machine written by: Chris Josephs
Illustrated by: John Harwood, Sally Launder, David Pratt,
Sylvia Treadgold

Designed by: Tri-Art
Series Editor: Christopher Tunney
Art Director: Keith Groom

Published by Christensen Press Limited, The Grange,
Grange Yard, London SE1 3AG.
© Christensen Press Limited 1985

First published 1985
Revised edition 1990

Printed and bound by Graficas Reunidas, Madrid, Spain.

ISBN: 0 946994 06 4

EVERYDAY Science

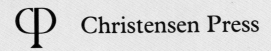 Christensen Press

What is science?

Science is concerned with how we collect, record, and organize the facts and ideas we have about the things around us. It is also about how we solve problems, the sort of experiments we set up to try to test our ideas, and the way our findings are used to develop and test new theories.

SCIENCE AND SCIENTISTS The ancient Greeks thought that all things were made of four basic materials—earth, air, fire, and water. This view persisted for hundreds of years. But few early scientists tried to prove their ideas right by experimenting. Only in the last 300 years or so have scientists tested their theories practically.

Isaac Newton

What kinds of questions do scientists ask?

Is it coloured all the way through? A very simple and crude experiment a scientist might perform to find the answer is to smash the rock with a hammer.

Is it hollow or is it solid? Is it hard or soft? How big is it? What is it made of? Will it burn? Are there others like it? Is it magnetic? Does it float in water? Will it change if treated with various chemicals? These are just some of the questions a scientist may ask if he finds something unusual.

What are the units of measurement?

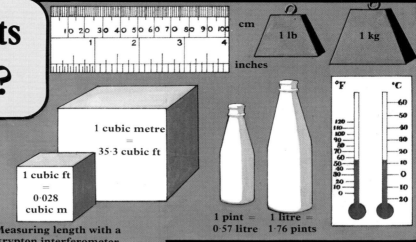

We find out how tall or wide or long or heavy things are by measuring them. Distance is measured in units such as metres and centimetres or feet and inches, weight in grams and kilograms or ounces and pounds.

1 cubic metre = 35·3 cubic ft

1 cubic ft = 0·028 cubic m

Measuring length with a krypton interferometer

1 pint = 0·57 litre

1 litre = 1·76 pints

Standard kilogram

cubit
7 palms
4 digits
1 palm
1 foot

In ancient times, people used parts of the body as standards of measurement. But these, of course, varied considerably. The International Bureau of Weights and Measures was founded in 1875 in France. There they keep, for example, a standard kilogram, made of a special alloy of platinum and iridium, and each member country has a duplicate. The standard metre is now based on the wavelength of light given off by krypton gas.

Why is measurement important?

In scientific experiments and in many everyday situations, it is important to use set amounts of materials. Even in making a cake, the ingredients have to be measured carefully. And a cake has to be cooked for a set time at a particular temperature.

Combining Measurements

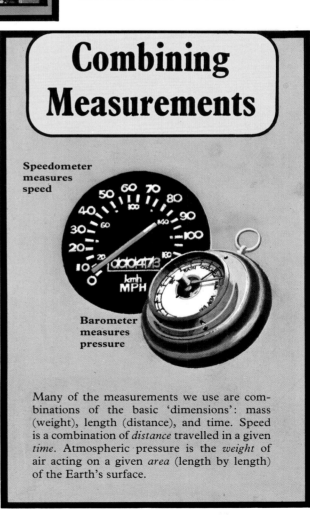

Speedometer measures speed

Barometer measures pressure

Many of the measurements we use are combinations of the basic 'dimensions': mass (weight), length (distance), and time. Speed is a combination of *distance* travelled in a given *time*. Atmospheric pressure is the *weight* of air acting on a given *area* (length by length) of the Earth's surface.

What is the difference between solids, liquids, and gases?

SOLIDS, LIQUIDS, AND GASES All known substances exist as solids, liquids, or gases in their normal state. The air around us is a mixture of gases. If you blow up a balloon, the air will take its shape. Pour wine into a glass, and the wine will take the shape of the glass. Neither the air (a gas) nor the wine (a liquid) has a definite shape of its own. Solids have.

SOLIDS

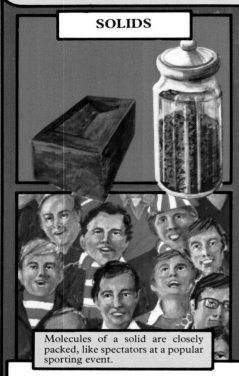

Molecules of a solid are closely packed, like spectators at a popular sporting event.

The molecules making up solids are packed tightly together, so solids have a shape of their own. Liquids have more space between their molecules, which are freer to move. Liquids do not have a definite shape of their own, though they have a definite size. Gases have even more widely spaced molecules, and can expand to any size.

LIQUIDS

Molecules of a liquid are freer to move, like dancers in a ballroom.

GASES

Molecules of a gas are free to move in all directions. They may collide occasionally.

Can the same thing have more than one state?

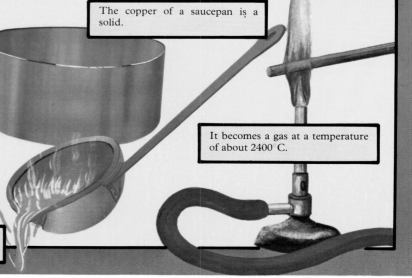

The copper of a saucepan is a solid.

It becomes a gas at a temperature of about 2400°C.

Most substances can exist as solids, liquids, and gases under certain conditions. At normal temperatures, copper is a solid, but when heated to 1083°C it melts to become a liquid. At a much higher temperature, it vaporizes (boils) and becomes a gas. On the other hand, carbon dioxide exists normally as a gas, but can be liquefied (turned into a liquid) at −56·6°C and then frozen into a solid at −78·5°C.

Copper becomes a liquid when heated to 1083°C.

What makes things change their state?

If you cool water below its freezing point, it will change into ice. Heat water until it boils, and it changes into steam, a gas. So water exists as a solid, liquid, and gas, depending on how hot or cold it is. Pressure can also bring about a change of state. Press hard on a block of ice, as with a skate, and the ice will gradually melt, even though it is still below freezing point.

Why do some things float in water?

Cork

Wood

Steel

A piece of cork or wood floats in water, but a piece of steel sinks. Yet a steel ship floats. Why? Place a model boat in a bowl of water, and the water level rises. The boat displaces its own weight of water, and so it floats. Fill the boat with water and it will sink. It cannot now displace the combined weight.

A ship floats as long as it displaces its own weight of water.

How a Submarine Surfaces and Dives

Submarines can cruise on the surface or dive deep underwater. They have tanks in the hull that are empty when the ship is on the surface. For diving, the tanks are flooded so that the submarine loses much of its buoyancy and sinks in the water. For surfacing, the water is blown out by compressed air.

What is an element?

An element is the simplest form of a substance—it cannot be separated into simpler substances that still have the same properties. Gold, mercury, carbon, iron, lead, copper, sulphur, zinc, oxygen, and hydrogen are examples. All substances are made up from elements.

BUILDING BLOCKS Elements are the building blocks of which the universe is made. Over one hundred elements have been identified on Earth. Some are hard, some soft, some are strong, others brittle. Two, bromine and mercury, exist normally as liquids. Eleven, such as hydrogen and helium, are normally gases. The rest are solids. Some rarely exist alone, being nearly always found in combination with others.

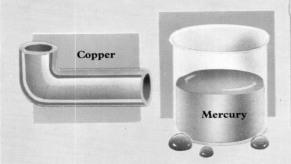

Copper

Mercury

Hydrogen in balloon

Zinc

Diamond (carbon)

Graphite (carbon)

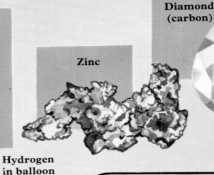

Mercury

Mercury oxide

On heating, mercury combines with oxygen

Separating iron filings from a mixture of iron and sulphur.

What happens when elements combine?

When gold occurs in a mixture, it can be separated by 'panning'.

Are metals elements?

Gold

Tungsten filament

Copper

Zinc

Brass

Aluminium

Yes, and most of the elements are metals. They look glossy, are good conductors of heat and electricity, and can be drawn out into wire and shaped by hammering. Some elements, such as arsenic, have some but not all of these properties. Metals can be mixed to form *alloys*. Brass, for example, is an alloy of copper and zinc.

The element mercury is a shiny, silver-coloured liquid. When heated, it combines with oxygen in the air to form a red powder, mercury oxide, a *compound* of mercury. Elements put together do not always combine to form compounds, however. In a *mixture*, the elements can be separated by physical means. Gold, for example, can be separated from rock particles.

Can elements be changed into other elements?

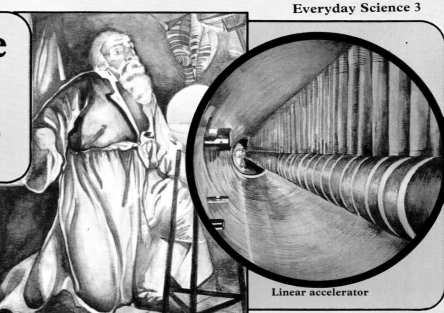

Linear accelerator

For many years people tried to change one element into another. The early chemists, called alchemists, attempted to make gold from other substances, but they were unsuccessful. We now know that radioactive elements such as uranium change into other elements. Huge *linear accelerators* are used to split elements—for example, gold can be made from mercury.

How many elements are there?

Ninety-two elements occur naturally on Earth. At least a dozen others have been made artificially by man. This is done in giant machines in which nuclear particles are accelerated to very high speeds so that they can break up the atoms of some elements, so changing them into other elements. In the 1800s, the Russian scientist Dmitri Mendeleyev arranged the elements in groups in what is called the Periodic Table.

The modern Periodic Table developed from Mendeleyev's work. Based on their atomic numbers (the number of protons), the elements fall into several groups, such as the so-called 'light metals', in yellow on the left, the 'heavy metals' in the centre (light brown), the non-metals (rust-coloured, on right), and the rare gases (far right, in red).

Hydrogen H 1																	Helium He 2
Lithium Li 3	Beryllium Be 4											Boron B 5	Carbon C 6	Nitrogen N 7	Oxygen O 8	Fluorine F 9	Neon Ne 10
Sodium Na 11	Magnesium Mg 12											Aluminium Al 13	Silicon Si 14	Phosphorus P 15	Sulphur S 16	Chlorine Cl 17	Argon Ar 18
Potassium K 19	Calcium Ca 20	Scandium Sc 21	Titanium Ti 22	Vanadium V 23	Chromium Cr 24	Manganese Mn 25	Iron Fe 26	Cobalt Co 27	Nickel Ni 28	Copper Cu 29	Zinc Zn 30	Gallium Ga 31	Germanium Ge 32	Arsenic As 33	Selenium Se 34	Bromine Br 35	Krypton Kr 36
Rubidium Rb 37	Strontium Sr 38	Yttrium Y 39	Zirconium Zr 40	Niobium Nb 41	Molybdenum Mo 42	Technetium Tc 43	Ruthenium Ru 44	Rhodium Rh 45	Palladium Pd 46	Silver Ag 47	Cadmium Cd 48	Indium In 49	Tin Sn 50	Antimony Sb 51	Tellurium Te 52	Iodine I 53	Xenon Xe 54
Caesium Cs 55	Barium Ba 56	Lanthanum La 57	Hafnium Hf 72	Tantalum Ta 73	Tungsten W 74	Rhenium Re 75	Osmium Os 76	Iridium Ir 77	Platinum Pt 78	Gold Au 79	Mercury Hg 80	Thallium Tl 81	Lead Pb 82	Bismuth Bi 83	Polonium Po 84	Astatine At 85	Radon Rn 86
Francium Fr 87	Radium Ra 88	Actinium Ac 89															

Rare earths	Cerium Ce 58	Praseodymium Pr 59	Neodymium Nd 60	Promethium Pm 61	Samarium Sm 62	Europium Eu 63	Gadolinium Gd 64	Terbium Tb 65	Dysprosium Dy 66	Holmium Ho 67	Erbium Er 68	Thulium Tm 69	Ytterbium Yb 70	Lutetium Lu 71	
Actinides	Thorium Th 90	Protactinium Pa 91	Uranium U 92	Neptunium Np 93	Plutonium Pu 94	Americium Am 95	Curium Cm 96	Berkelium Bk 97	Californium Cf 98	Einsteinium Es 99	Fermium Fm 100	Mendelevium Md 101	Nobelium No 102	Lawrencium Lr 103	**?**

What are atoms made of?

ATOMS All the chemical elements that make up the many different substances are quite distinct. Gold differs from silver, and silver from carbon. But what makes them different? Each element is made up of tiny particles called atoms. These do not change during chemical changes. Atoms combine in fixed proportions when compounds are formed. They are the smallest pieces of an element that can take part in a chemical reaction.

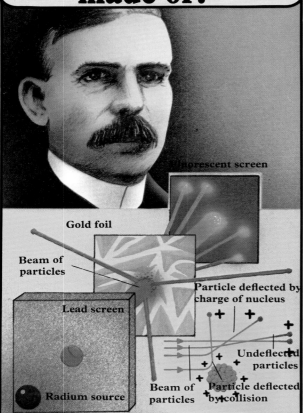

Fluorescent screen

Gold foil

Beam of particles

Lead screen

Particle deflected by charge of nucleus

Undeflected particles

Radium source

Beam of particles

Particle deflected by collision

British physicist Lord Rutherford was one of the first to demonstrate the nature of the atom.

All the elements are made up of atoms. The atoms of different elements are composed of identical tiny particles. But these vary in number from one element to another. The centre, or *nucleus*, consists of *protons* and *neutrons*, with *electrons* circling round them. Protons have a positive electrical charge, electrons negative. Rutherford was one of the first to demonstrate the true nature of the atom. He fired a stream of charged particles (alpha-particles) at a sheet of gold foil. Most particles passed straight through, while only a few were deflected or bounced back. He concluded that the atom (of gold in this case) was mostly empty space, with a solid nucleus and orbiting electrons.

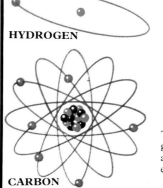

HYDROGEN

HELIUM

CARBON

These are simplified diagrams of atoms. There are always the same number of electrons as protons.

Are all atoms of one element the same?

Many elements exist in more than one form, each with the same number of protons but a different number of neutrons. Hydrogen has three 'versions', or *isotopes*: hydrogen, deuterium, and tritium.

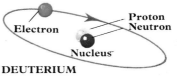

HYDROGEN

Electron

Proton
Neutron

Nucleus

DEUTERIUM

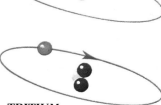

TRITIUM

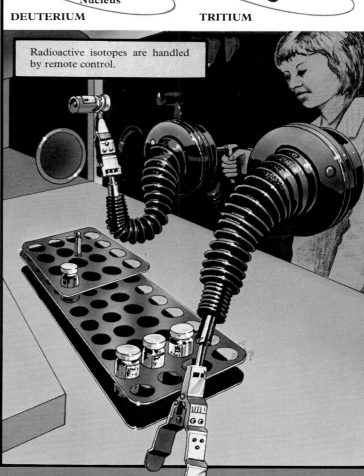

Radioactive isotopes are handled by remote control.

How do atoms combine?

When elements combine, their atoms share some of their electrons. The compound produced has different properties from its constituent elements. Sodium and chlorine, for example, are reactive and unpleasant alone, but they combine to form salt, a harmless substance.

By itself, chlorine is a suffocating poisonous gas.

Sodium, a metal, reacts violently with water.

$$2Na + Cl_2 = 2NaCl$$

Sodium (Na) combines with chlorine (Cl) to form the compound sodium chloride (NaCl)

Salt, which consists of sodium and chlorine, is harmless and an important part of our diet.

What happens when an atom splits?

Neutron

A nuclear chain reaction: Uranium atoms are split by collision with neutrons.

Uranium atom

The atom bomb—an uncontrolled chain reaction.

When an atom splits, there is a rearrangement of the neutrons and protons. As a result, a nuclear reaction takes place, and a lot of heat energy is released. The splitting, or *fission*, of uranium can be controlled in a nuclear reactor so that the heat can be used to produce electricity.

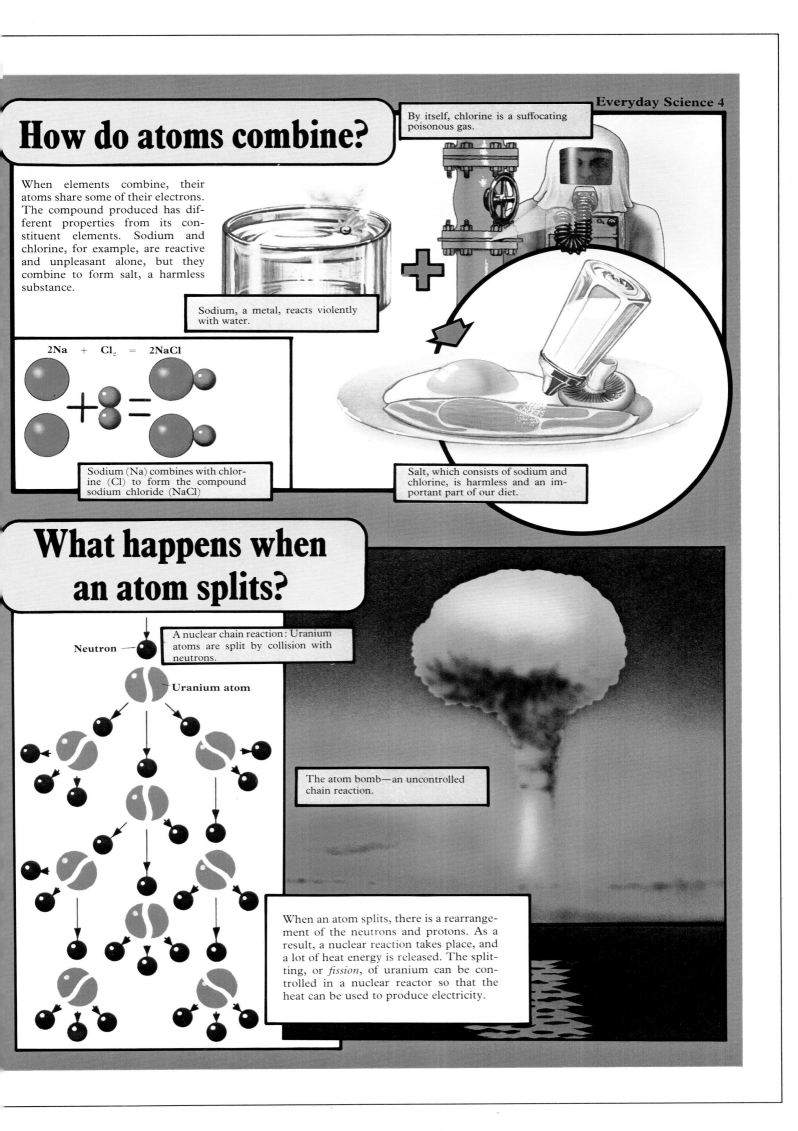

What is light?

LIGHT We see an object because light reaching the eyes has been reflected from it. Some ancient Greeks thought that light consisted of tiny corpuscles. Others thought differently, but all knew that it travelled in straight lines. In the 1600s, the English scientist Robert Hooke proposed a wave theory. More modern views suggest that it is a mixture of the two—wave and particle.

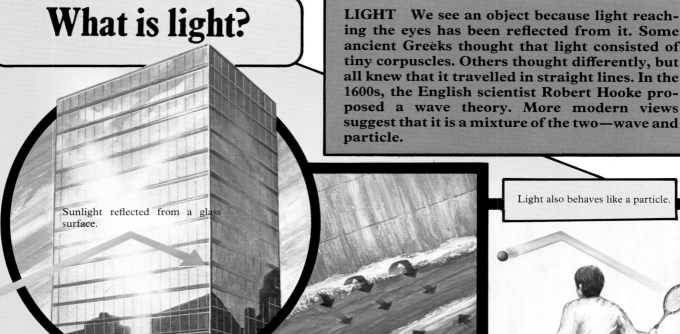

Sunlight reflected from a glass surface.

Light behaves like a wave.

Light also behaves like a particle.

A mirror held up to the sun gives a dazzling reflection. The light behaves in some ways like a sea wave reflected back off a quay. But it also acts like a ball (or particle) rebounding from a wall. Light can also cause chemical changes and produce electric currents. One thing is certain—it is a form of energy.

How fast does it travel?

Light travels at a speed of about 300,000 km (186,000 miles) per second. For this reason, it takes the light from the Sun $8\frac{1}{2}$ minutes to reach us on Earth. The most accurate measurements of the speed of light have been made with lasers and with microwave aerials (above), which send and receive highly directional beams.

Can we measure it?

Dull day

Bright day

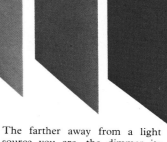

The brightness of light is measured in units called *candelas*. An ordinary 40-watt bulb has a brightness of 35 candelas. A light meter, as used in photography, measures the light falling on a light-sensitive surface (a photoelectric cell) in electrical terms.

The farther away from a light source you are, the dimmer its light.

How does a mirror reflect light?

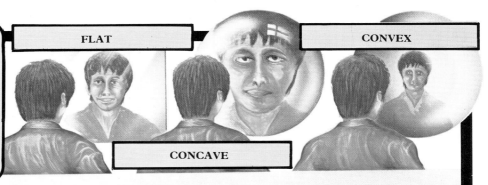

FLAT

CONCAVE

CONVEX

A mirror is a bright surface that does not absorb light rays but reflects them. When you look in a flat mirror, the left side of your face appears to be on the right, your right on the left. Curved mirrors produce images of different sizes compared with flat mirrors. The diagrams show how these images are formed.

Image

Focus

Object

Concave mirror

An object placed inside the focus of a concave mirror produces a larger image.

Focus Image Convex mirror Object

An object in front of a convex mirror produces a smaller image.

What happens when light travels through water?

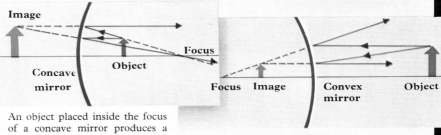

The bending of light from air to water can cause errors of judgement!

When light rays enter water from air at an angle, they are *refracted* (bent or deflected). This makes objects in water look nearer than they really are. An angler, for example, when landing a fish, might misjudge the exact position of the fish in the water. Place a straw in a glass half full of water, and you will see what we mean.

... and through glass?

Light rays are bent when they pass from one medium (type of substance) to another because the speed of light is changed. Thus, just as they bend when passing from air to water, they bend when passing from air to glass. This is how lenses work. Even a thin pane of glass can distort the view through a window if it is uneven. But if the surfaces of the glass are parallel, the rays of light emerge at the same angle as they entered, having been bent back again when passing from glass to air.

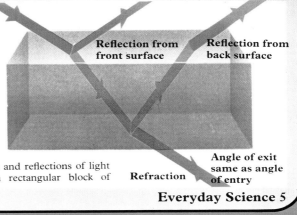

Reflection from front surface

Reflection from back surface

Refraction and reflections of light through a rectangular block of glass.

Refraction

Angle of exit same as angle of entry

Everyday Science 5

How does a magnifying glass magnify?

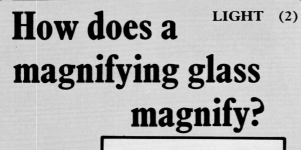

A magnifying glass produces an enlarged image of the object.

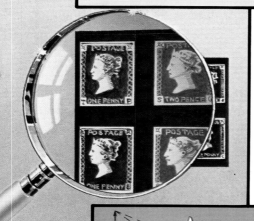

Focusing the Sun's rays to burn a hole in paper.

A ray diagram showing how the Sun's rays are concentrated at the focus of the lens.

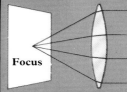

Focus

A ray diagram showing how an object (O) is seen as an enlarged image (I).

A magnifying glass is a kind of lens. Its surfaces curve outwards—they are *convex*. The lens is fatter in the middle than at the edges. Light rays have to travel farther through the thick part, and this bends them so that they are brought to a *focus*—they concentrate together. As a result, the rays of light reaching the eye seem to be coming from an object larger than it really is.

How do spectacles help you to see?

Your eyes may be too short or too long from front to back, or the lens of the eye may not be able to change shape sufficiently for you to be able to focus properly. You may be able to see near or distant objects clearly, but not both. The eye is said to be short-sighted or long-sighted, respectively. A spectacle lens or contact lens of the right shape can make up for the eye's defects by focusing the light rays at the back of the eye.

Rays brought to focus behind retina

Corrected by convex lens

Rays brought to focus in front of retina

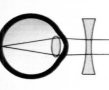

Corrected by concave lens

What is colour?

A prism splits up white light into the colours of the spectrum.

A red pencil reflects only the red part of white light.

When white light passes through a prism, it is split up into its colours. The different colours making up white light are bent a different amount, and so they are seen as the colours of the spectrum. When light falls on an object, some colours may be absorbed while others are reflected. Black objects absorb all the light. White objects reflect all the light.

How is a rainbow formed?

How light is refracted and reflected by a raindrop.

White light

A raindrop acts as a prism, splitting up white light into its colours. The bent rays are reflected from the inside of the raindrop, and bent more on leaving it. So a rainbow is produced when the sun shines on raindrops in the sky.

What are the primary colours?

A white object looks white because all the colours of white light are reflected. A shirt appears to change from white to red in the red spotlight, because there is only red light to be reflected. Red, blue, and green spotlights can be combined to give white light or any colour. They are called the primary colours.

The primary colours in light are red, blue, and green.

The primary colours in pigments are special shades of red, blue, and yellow.

Red, blue, and green light combine to produce white light.

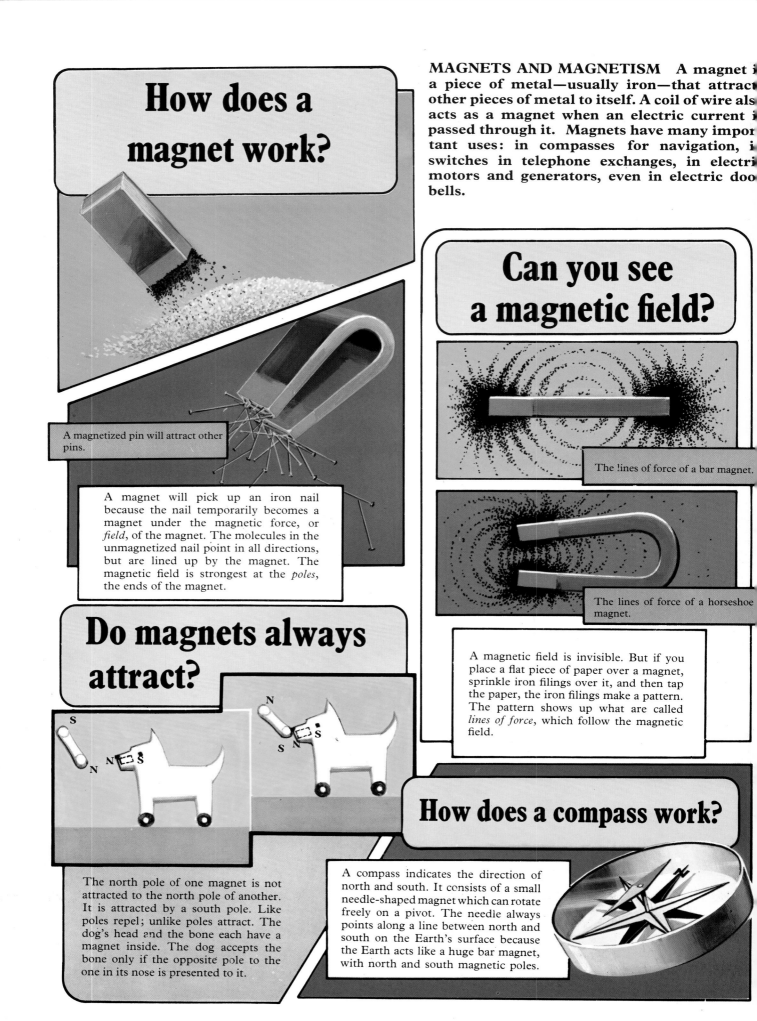

How does a magnet work?

MAGNETS AND MAGNETISM A magnet i a piece of metal—usually iron—that attract other pieces of metal to itself. A coil of wire als acts as a magnet when an electric current i passed through it. Magnets have many impor tant uses: in compasses for navigation, i switches in telephone exchanges, in electri motors and generators, even in electric doo bells.

A magnetized pin will attract other pins.

A magnet will pick up an iron nail because the nail temporarily becomes a magnet under the magnetic force, or *field*, of the magnet. The molecules in the unmagnetized nail point in all directions, but are lined up by the magnet. The magnetic field is strongest at the *poles*, the ends of the magnet.

Can you see a magnetic field?

The lines of force of a bar magnet.

The lines of force of a horseshoe magnet.

A magnetic field is invisible. But if you place a flat piece of paper over a magnet, sprinkle iron filings over it, and then tap the paper, the iron filings make a pattern. The pattern shows up what are called *lines of force*, which follow the magnetic field.

Do magnets always attract?

The north pole of one magnet is not attracted to the north pole of another. It is attracted by a south pole. Like poles repel; unlike poles attract. The dog's head and the bone each have a magnet inside. The dog accepts the bone only if the opposite pole to the one in its nose is presented to it.

How does a compass work?

A compass indicates the direction of north and south. It consists of a small needle-shaped magnet which can rotate freely on a pivot. The needle always points along a line between north and south on the Earth's surface because the Earth acts like a huge bar magnet, with north and south magnetic poles.

Where are the Earth's magnetic poles?

A bar magnet suspended on a string so that it hangs horizontally and swings freely always comes to rest pointing the same way. If this were repeated over the Earth's surface, the magnets would be seen to point along the Earth's lines of force. The Earth has a north and south magnetic pole, which are not the same as the geographic poles, as can be seen from the map.

The north magnetic pole is 74 N 100 W; the south is 67 S 142 W.

A gyrocompass is used on ships as an aid to navigation.

North magnetic pole

South magnetic pole

How does magnetic tape work?

The dull side of a magnetic tape is coated with special paste containing iron or chromium oxide crystals. These act like hundreds of tiny magnets. When a recording is being made, these are formed into a magnetic pattern representing the sound. The playback head reacts to the magnetic pattern on the tape producing electric currents that are changed into sound again.

Magnetic tape

Erase head

Record head

Playback head

Unaligned magnets

Aligned after passing erase head

Pattern after recording

Pattern reproduced by playback

What causes lightning?

KINDS OF ELECTRICITY You cannot see electricity, but you can see that it provides light and heat, for example. The kind of electricity that flows through wires is current electricity. Sometimes you receive a mild shock when getting out of a car. This is because a still form of electricity—static electricity—has built up on you as you rub against the car seat. It is earthed when you touch the metal of the car door with your feet on the ground.

Lightning is static electricity caused by a build-up of electrons on clouds. Clouds become negatively charged owing to the friction between water droplets and ice crystals tossed about in a thundercloud. The Earth becomes positively charged. Eventually a stream of electrons moves from the cloud towards the Earth in the form of lightning.

What is static electricity?

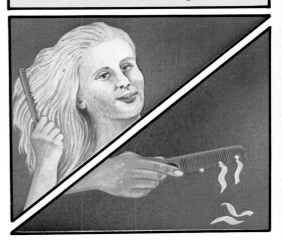

Run a plastic comb through your hair, and then place the comb near some small pieces of paper. The pieces will fly up to the comb. They are attracted to the comb because the comb is charged electrically by rubbing against your hair. It attracts electrons to it from the hair. The build-up of charge is static electricity.

How does a lightning conductor work?

A lightning conductor is a metal strip, usually copper, reaching from the roof down to the ground. The spike at the top becomes positive when a negatively charged cloud passes above it, and it usually makes the cloud lose its charge slowly and safely. But if lightning does strike, it is discharged to Earth harmlessly down the conductor.

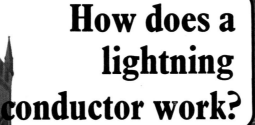

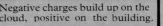
Negative charges build up on the cloud, positive on the building.

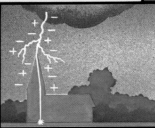
A lightning conductor discharges lightning safely to earth.

What is an electric current?

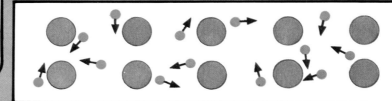

No current—electrons moving at random.

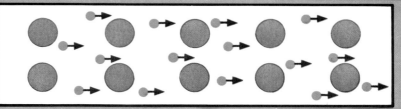

Current flowing—electrons moving in same direction.

Current electricity is a moving stream of electrons jumping from atom to atom. It moves most easily through conductors—copper and aluminium, for example. (Static electricity builds up best on non-conductors, such as wood and plastic.) When a torch is switched on, the circuit is completed between the positive and negative terminals. Electrons flow from negative to positive through to the bulb, which lights up.

The electric circuit of a torch. The circuit is completed when the switch joins two brass strips inside the casing. One brass strip leads to the bulb, the other to a spring, which leads through the batteries (cells) to the bulb again.

Brass strip makes contact

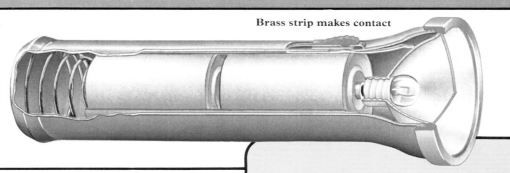

Cells and Batteries

In a wet cell, two metals, such as copper and zinc, are placed in water containing a salt—the electrolyte. If the metals are connected by a wire, electrons flow from zinc to copper.

When a cell is used to produce electricity, chemical changes take place, and the chemicals in the cell are used up. In a *primary cell*, such as a torch battery, these changes usually cannot be reversed. Eventually the cell runs down, and has to be thrown away. But a *secondary cell*, such as a car battery, can be recharged by passing an electric current through it to reverse the chemical changes.

Copper rod

Zinc rod

+ −

Electrolyte (copper sulphate solution)

In a dry cell, a carbon rod is surrounded by chemical paste in a zinc can. When a connection is made between the carbon and the zinc, electrons flow from zinc to carbon via a bulb.

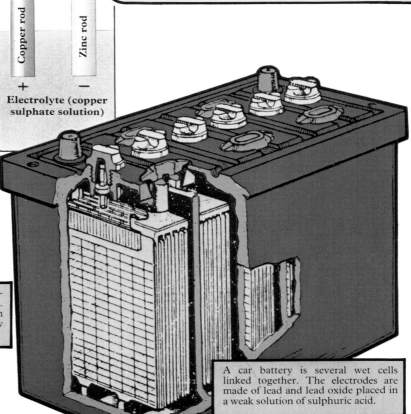

Carbon electrode

Zinc case

Paper lining

Chemical paste

A car battery is several wet cells linked together. The electrodes are made of lead and lead oxide placed in a weak solution of sulphuric acid.

How is electricity made, distributed, and used?

AC AND DC Current electricity can be made chemically in a dry cell or wet cell. We use cells in cars, torches, and radios. The electricity they produce flows in one direction only—it is direct current (DC). The electricity we use in our homes and factories is made in power stations by turbogenerators. It flows backwards and forwards along the wires, and is called alternating current (AC).

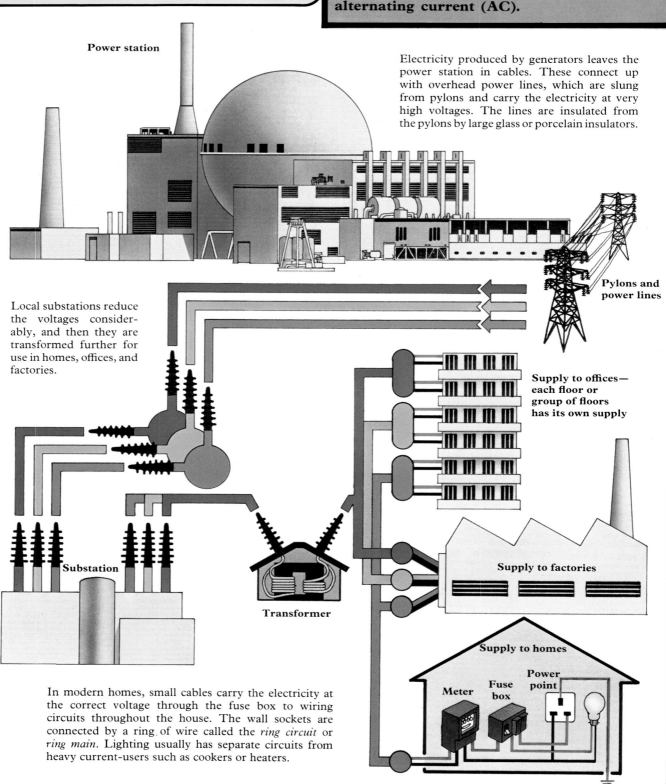

Power station

Electricity produced by generators leaves the power station in cables. These connect up with overhead power lines, which are slung from pylons and carry the electricity at very high voltages. The lines are insulated from the pylons by large glass or porcelain insulators.

Pylons and power lines

Local substations reduce the voltages considerably, and then they are transformed further for use in homes, offices, and factories.

Supply to offices—each floor or group of floors has its own supply

Substation

Transformer

Supply to factories

Supply to homes

Power point

Meter

Fuse box

In modern homes, small cables carry the electricity at the correct voltage through the fuse box to wiring circuits throughout the house. The wall sockets are connected by a ring of wire called the *ring circuit* or *ring main*. Lighting usually has separate circuits from heavy current-users such as cookers or heaters.

How does a generator work?

If a coil of wire moves in a magnetic field, an electric current flows through a circuit connecting the ends of the wire in the coil. In a generator, the magnetic field is created in a coil—the field coil. Several field coils are arranged round moving coils, so that large currents can be made. The generator is turned by a water or steam turbine.

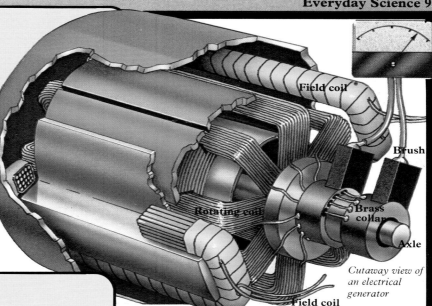

Cutaway view of an electrical generator

Field coil

Brush

Brass collar

Axle

Rotating coil

Field coil

What is an electricity meter?

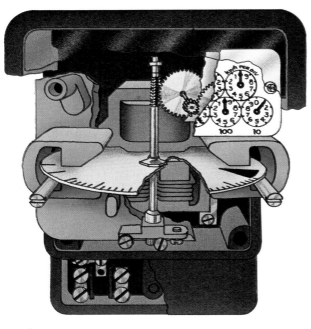

An electricity meter is a sort of electric motor. It has a horizontal disk which turns when an electric light or appliance is switched on. The disk's speed increases as more electricity is used. As it turns, it moves a group of pointers or rotates numbers to which it is connected by gears. As the pointers move over their dials, the amount of electricity used can be read off the dials.

Why do we use fuses?

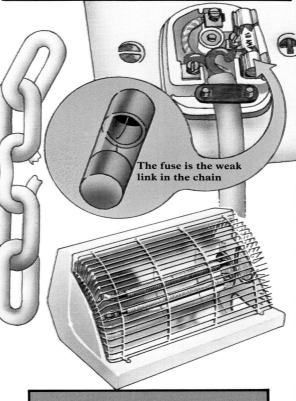

The fuse is the weak link in the chain

A wire carrying an electric current becomes hot, depending on how much it resists the flow of electrons—this is called its *electrical resistance*. A fuse is a short length of wire with a low resistance. If too much current flows, it melts and breaks the circuit. It protects other parts of the circuit.

How does sound travel?

SOUND Sound gives us pleasure and it annoys. It can be loud or soft, high or low—so low o high that we are unable to hear it, even thoug some animals can. It can echo like a ball bounc ing off a wall. If a wagon at the end of a line o railway wagons bumps into the next one, th effects of the bump move along the line fror wagon to wagon. Sound travels with this kin of motion, and it travels at a high speed.

Sound travels in waves rather like the ripples on a pond.

When a guitar string is plucked, it moves to and fro—it vibrates—and you hear a sound. The molecules in the air surrounding the moving string are pushed and pulled, and this pushes and pulls more molecules. So the sound spreads through the air until it reaches your ears. Sound can travel through liquids and solids too, but not through a vacuum, because there are no molecules to vibrate in a vacuum.

The speed of sound in air is about 335 metres per second (1,100 ft/sec). In water, it is over 4 times as fast, and in iron 15 times as fast. It travels faster at higher temperatures, but slower at heights, because there are fewer molecules to vibrate.

How fast does it travel?

After the plane has crossed the 'sound barrier', it leaves the pressure wave behind. The shock wave spreads out and reaches the ground to be heard as a sonic boom.

Pressure waves are created round the flying plane. They travel at the speed of sound.

As it reaches the speed of sound, the plane catches up with the pressure waves and a shock wave builds up.

What is an echo?

A theatre is designed so that there is a balance between wanted and unwanted echoes.

If you are in an empty room or a long, narrow alleyway, your voice will echo off the walls. The sound waves bounce back so that you hear both your voice and then its echo. Smooth, hard surfaces produce the best echoes. In a confined space such as a theatre, the sound of music or voices echoes off the walls. Echoes can be reduced by the use of materials that absorb sound. But it is necessary in a theatre or concert hall to have enough echo for sound to carry well.

An alpine horn will produce echoes in a mountain region.

The Sonar System

Some ships employ sonar, an instrument that uses echoes. It stands for *s*ound *n*avigation *a*nd *r*anging. Sounds are sent through the water at regular intervals. They bounce off underwater objects, perhaps another ship or a shoal of fish. The time that the echo takes to return shows how far away the object is.

A warship uses its sonar to detect enemy craft such as submarines.

A metal disk is made from the vinyl impression and then thousands of plastic records can be produced.

Vibrations produced by the singer's voice are used to make a needle vibrate and cut a groove in a vinyl disk.

How is sound recorded?

In making records, sound vibrations are changed into electrical impulses, which cause a needle to vibrate and cut a groove in a vinyl disk. When a disk copied from this is played, the needle of the record player causes a crystal to vibrate. This produces electric currents that are changed into sound.

The record is played on the record player. The needle vibrates in the groove creating electrical impulses.

The impulses are used to create sound, which is relayed through the loudspeaker.

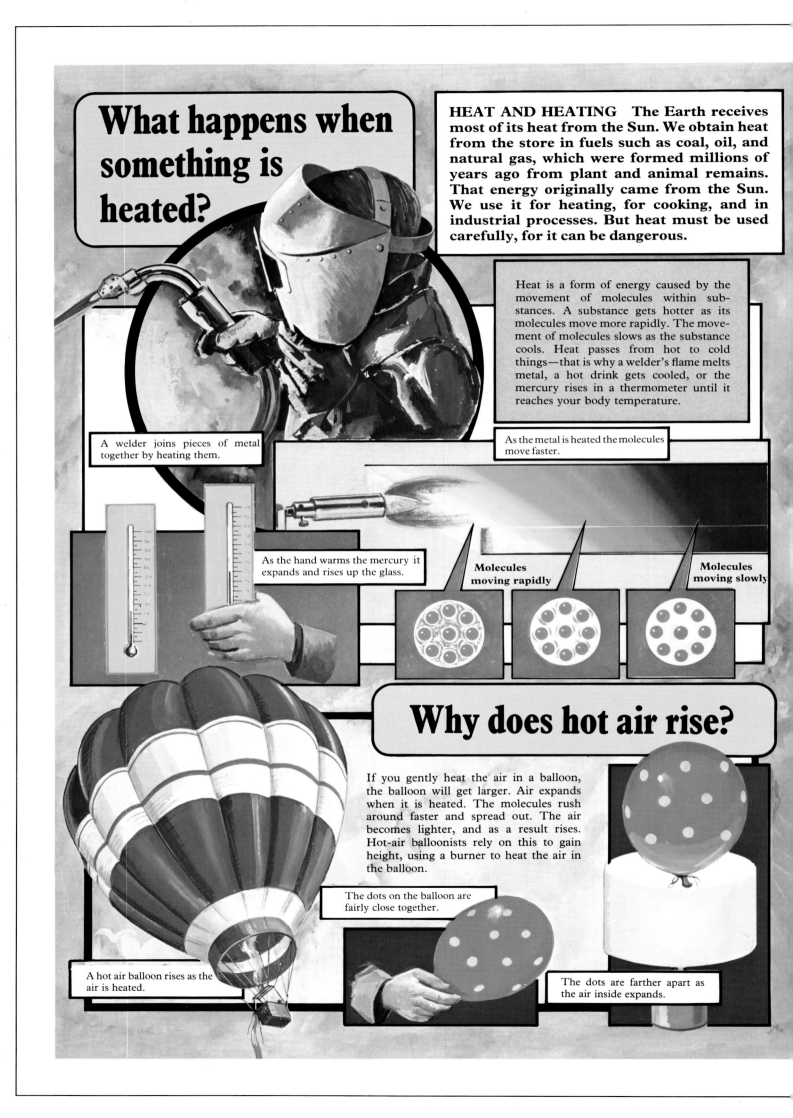

What happens when something is heated?

HEAT AND HEATING The Earth receives most of its heat from the Sun. We obtain heat from the store in fuels such as coal, oil, and natural gas, which were formed millions of years ago from plant and animal remains. That energy originally came from the Sun. We use it for heating, for cooking, and in industrial processes. But heat must be used carefully, for it can be dangerous.

Heat is a form of energy caused by the movement of molecules within substances. A substance gets hotter as its molecules move more rapidly. The movement of molecules slows as the substance cools. Heat passes from hot to cold things—that is why a welder's flame melts metal, a hot drink gets cooled, or the mercury rises in a thermometer until it reaches your body temperature.

A welder joins pieces of metal together by heating them.

As the metal is heated the molecules move faster.

As the hand warms the mercury it expands and rises up the glass.

Molecules moving rapidly

Molecules moving slowly

Why does hot air rise?

If you gently heat the air in a balloon, the balloon will get larger. Air expands when it is heated. The molecules rush around faster and spread out. The air becomes lighter, and as a result rises. Hot-air balloonists rely on this to gain height, using a burner to heat the air in the balloon.

The dots on the balloon are fairly close together.

A hot air balloon rises as the air is heated.

The dots are farther apart as the air inside expands.

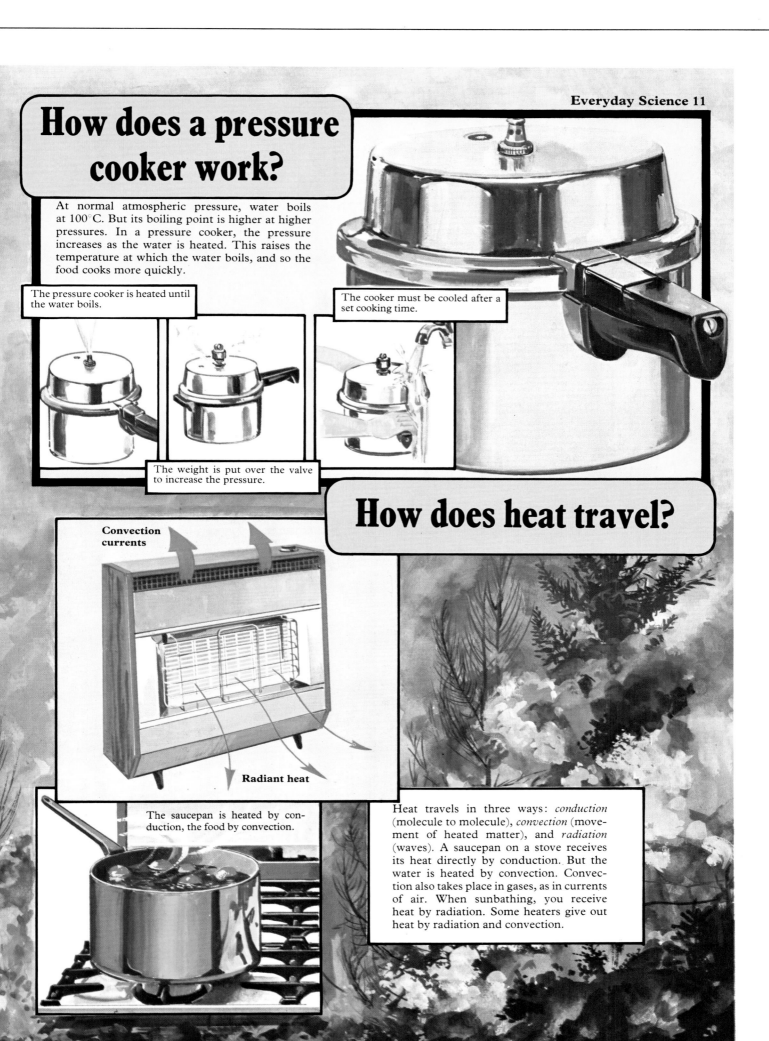

How does a pressure cooker work?

At normal atmospheric pressure, water boils at 100°C. But its boiling point is higher at higher pressures. In a pressure cooker, the pressure increases as the water is heated. This raises the temperature at which the water boils, and so the food cooks more quickly.

The pressure cooker is heated until the water boils.

The cooker must be cooled after a set cooking time.

The weight is put over the valve to increase the pressure.

How does heat travel?

Convection currents

Radiant heat

The saucepan is heated by conduction, the food by convection.

Heat travels in three ways: *conduction* (molecule to molecule), *convection* (movement of heated matter), and *radiation* (waves). A saucepan on a stove receives its heat directly by conduction. But the water is heated by convection. Convection also takes place in gases, as in currents of air. When sunbathing, you receive heat by radiation. Some heaters give out heat by radiation and convection.

What makes things move?

FORCES AND MOVEMENT If a car is driven into the back of a stationary car, it stops suddenly. The driver of the stationary car is jerked backwards. The crashing driver is thrown forwards, even though the car has stopped. The tendency for moving objects to keep on moving and for those at rest to stay still is called 'inertia'. The 'momentum' of a moving object is its mass times its velocity (speed and direction).

Forces make things move. Forces also cause things to stop or change direction. You move a billiard ball by applying force with a cue, a car by applying force with the engine. The speed and direction of a car can be changed only by applying a force—turning the steering wheel or braking, for example.

The driver of the crashing car is thrown forwards; the other driver is jerked backwards.

A moving ball transfers some of its momentum to a stationary ball.

Why do things fall?

The tightrope walker falls when his centre of gravity shifts to either side of the wire.

The tightrope walker uses his balancing pole to make sure that his *centre of gravity* is kept above the wire. Centre of gravity is the point at which the mass of an object seems to be concentrated. If the tightrope walker loses his balance and falls, it is because his centre of gravity is not directly above the wire. Gravity will then pull him downwards.

How fast do they fall?

If an object is dropped from the top of a tall building, it falls because the force of gravity pulls it down. As the object falls, it moves faster and faster each second—9·8 metres (32 ft) per second faster. Objects of different weights fall at the same rate. On Earth, air resistance slows down some objects more than others. But on the Moon, a stone and a feather would fall at the same rate.

½ sec

1 sec

1½ sec

2 sec

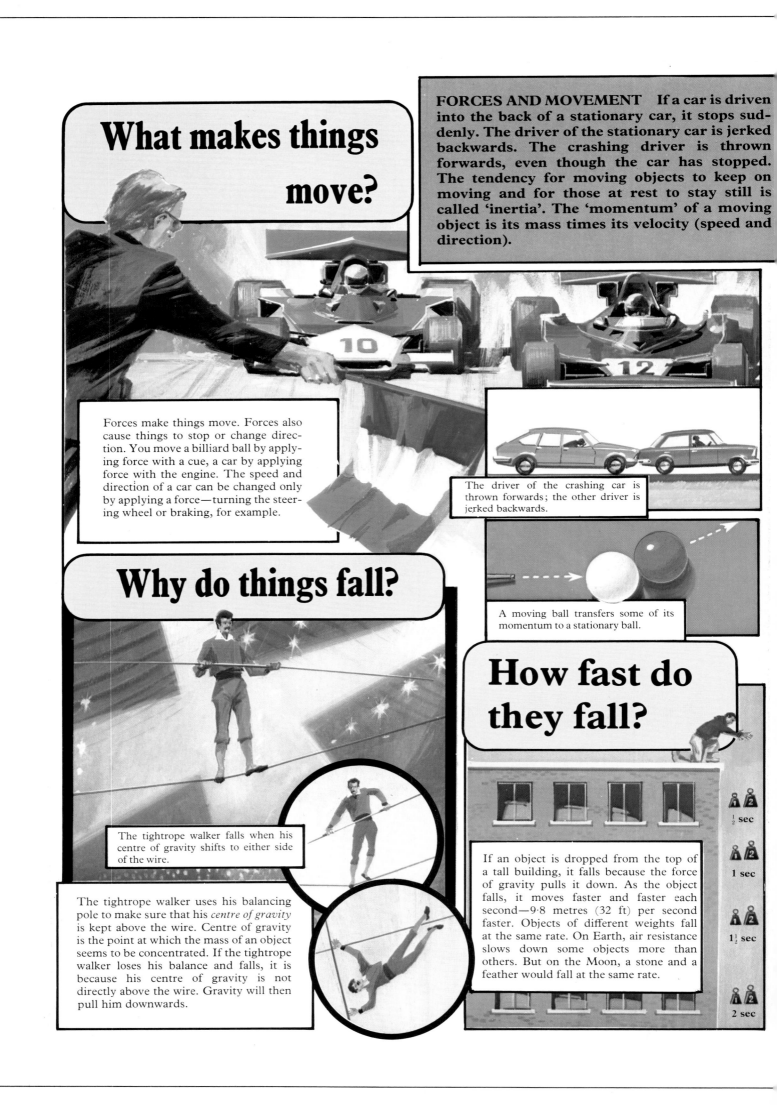

Motion in a Circle

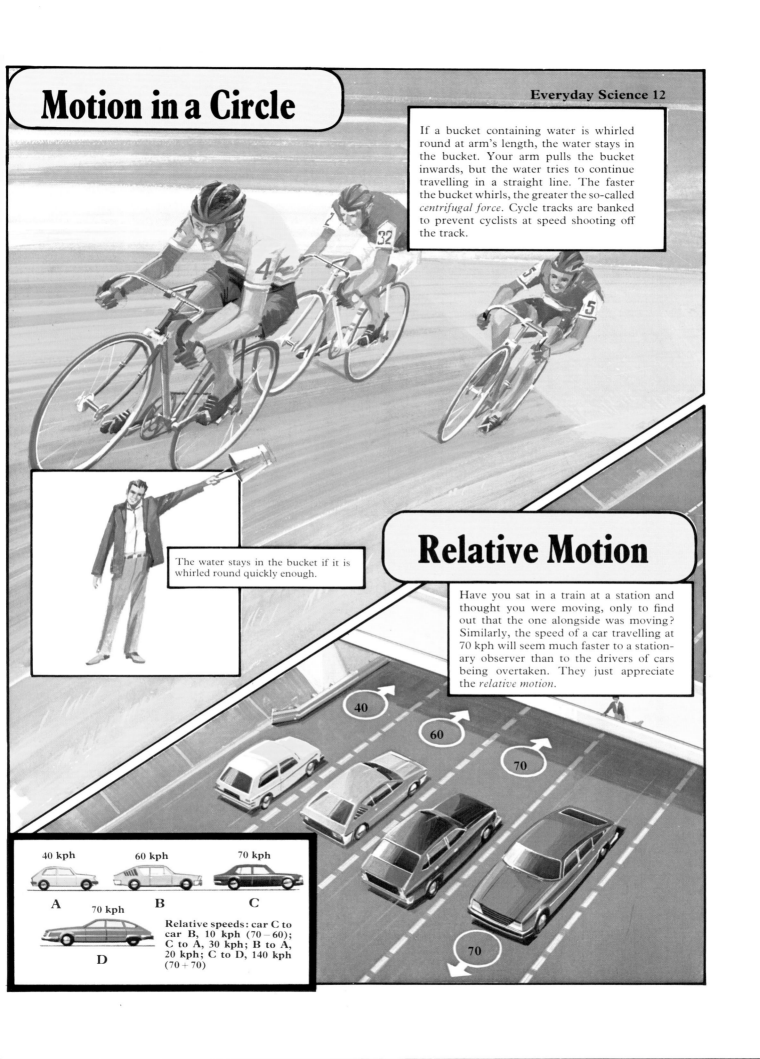

If a bucket containing water is whirled round at arm's length, the water stays in the bucket. Your arm pulls the bucket inwards, but the water tries to continue travelling in a straight line. The faster the bucket whirls, the greater the so-called *centrifugal force*. Cycle tracks are banked to prevent cyclists at speed shooting off the track.

The water stays in the bucket if it is whirled round quickly enough.

Relative Motion

Have you sat in a train at a station and thought you were moving, only to find out that the one alongside was moving? Similarly, the speed of a car travelling at 70 kph will seem much faster to a stationary observer than to the drivers of cars being overtaken. They just appreciate the *relative motion*.

40

60

70

70

40 kph

60 kph

70 kph

A

B

C

70 kph

D

Relative speeds: car C to car B, 10 kph (70 − 60); C to A, 30 kph; B to A, 20 kph; C to D, 140 kph (70 + 70)

ENERGY AND MACHINES If you run round a track or lift a heavy object, you are using energy. In lifting the load, you are doing work. Energy is the ability or capacity for doing work. We are very dependent on energy. We obtain our bodily energy from food. But most of the energy we need for working machines comes from fuel.

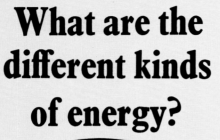

Kinetic energy of water flowing down a dam turns turbogenerators to produce electricity.

Energy is never created or destroyed. It is only changed in form. We change the chemical energy in the food we eat and the air we breathe into the kinetic energy (energy of movement) used for running (1). A steam locomotive (2) changes the chemical energy of fuel to the mechanical energy that turns the wheels. Other forms of energy include electrical energy, which may be changed to light energy (3); nuclear energy (4); and sound energy (5). Potential energy is stored energy, as in the water held back by a dam.

What is a machine?

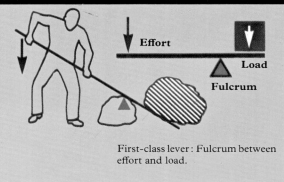

First-class lever: Fulcrum between effort and load.

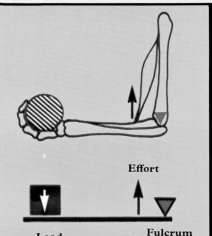

Effort

Load

Fulcrum

Third-class lever: Effort between fulcrum and load.

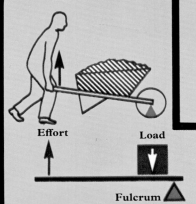

Effort

Load

Fulcrum

Second-class lever: Load between fulcrum and effort.

Any device, such as a lever, that enables energy to be used more easily is called a machine. Levers, for example, allow effort to be applied at one place to create movement at another. There are three classes of levers, depending on the position of *effort*, *load*, and *fulcrum* (point on which it rests).

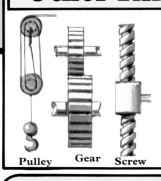

A simple crane uses the principles of the lever and the pulley.

Other Kinds of Machines

Pulley   **Gear**   **Screw**

A *lever* is probably the best-known type of simple machine. It is used, for example, in cranes, and these also make use of *pulleys*—another type of machine. Most pulley systems enable large weights to be moved by applying a smaller effort than the weight to be lifted. *Gears* enable an engine revolving at high speed to turn the wheels of a vehicle more slowly. A *screw* can also be used to the same effect, as in a car jack.

What is hydraulics?

If a fluid in a pipe is pushed by a piston, the force exerted on the fluid will act at the end of the pipe. The use of forces in liquids in this way is called *hydraulics*. It is a good way of spreading force evenly. It is used in machinery such as bulldozers, aircraft undercarriages, car brakes, and lifts.

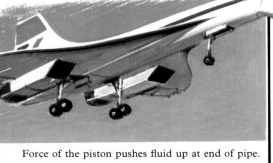

Force of the piston pushes fluid up at end of pipe.

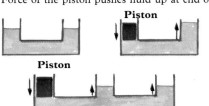

Piston

Piston

Piston

How do car brakes work?

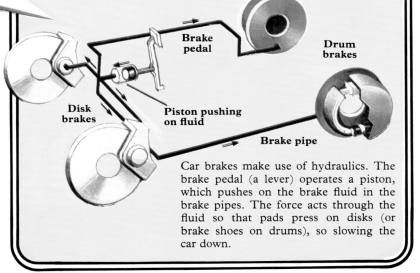

Brake pedal

Drum brakes

Disk brakes

Piston pushing on fluid

Brake pipe

Car brakes make use of hydraulics. The brake pedal (a lever) operates a piston, which pushes on the brake fluid in the brake pipes. The force acts through the fluid so that pads press on disks (or brake shoes on drums), so slowing the car down.

What's new in science?

An electronic pocket calculator—a spin-off from space research.

The need to conserve energy has led to the use of solar energy for heating houses.

A digital watch with a liquid crystal display showing the time. It can also show the day, date, and seconds.

Developments in electronics have made it possible to adapt a television set for numerous purposes.

Advances in drilling technology have enabled offshore platforms to extract oil and gas from under deep water.

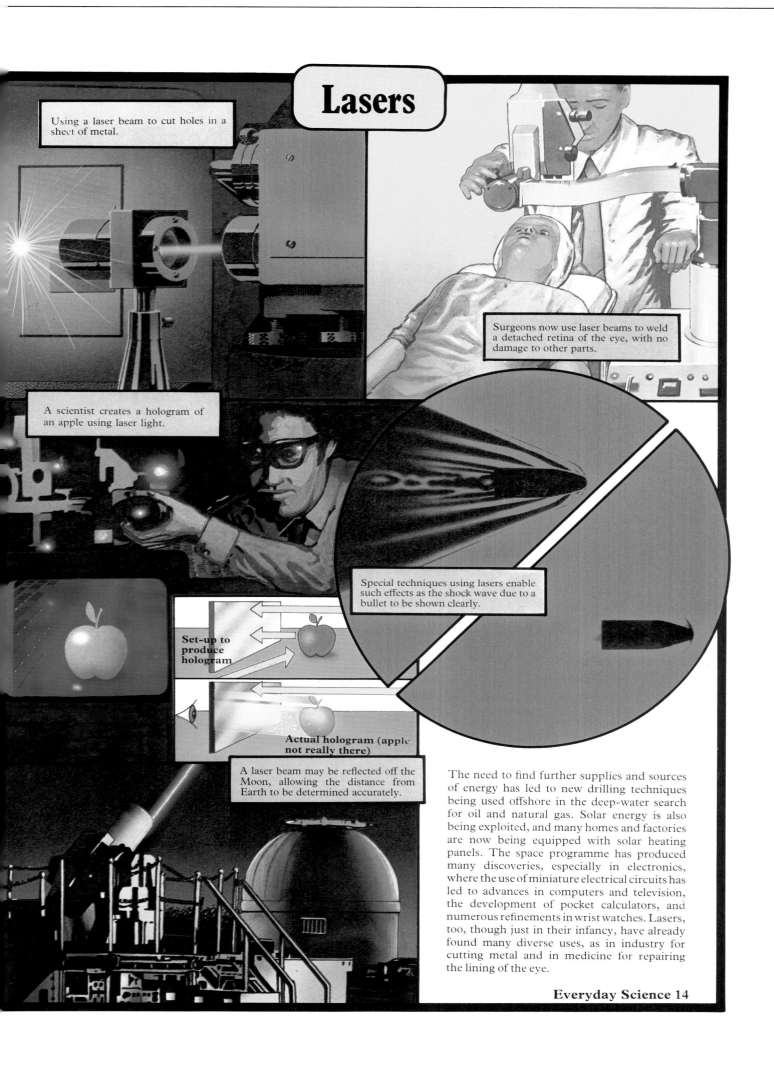

Lasers

Using a laser beam to cut holes in a sheet of metal.

Surgeons now use laser beams to weld a detached retina of the eye, with no damage to other parts.

A scientist creates a hologram of an apple using laser light.

Special techniques using lasers enable such effects as the shock wave due to a bullet to be shown clearly.

Set-up to produce hologram

Actual hologram (apple not really there)

A laser beam may be reflected off the Moon, allowing the distance from Earth to be determined accurately.

The need to find further supplies and sources of energy has led to new drilling techniques being used offshore in the deep-water search for oil and natural gas. Solar energy is also being exploited, and many homes and factories are now being equipped with solar heating panels. The space programme has produced many discoveries, especially in electronics, where the use of miniature electrical circuits has led to advances in computers and television, the development of pocket calculators, and numerous refinements in wrist watches. Lasers, too, though just in their infancy, have already found many diverse uses, as in industry for cutting metal and in medicine for repairing the lining of the eye.

A-Z of Science

A

absolute zero The lowest temperature that can be obtained theoretically—0° Absolute or −273·1°C.

air A mixture of gases that makes up the atmosphere surrounding the Earth. Nitrogen makes up 78% by volume, oxygen 21%, the remaining 1% being largely argon with smaller amounts of carbon dioxide, helium, neon, krypton, and xenon.

alloy A mixture of metals that has improved properties, such as strength and hardness, compared with the individual metals. Stainless steel is an alloy of iron and chromium, brass an alloy of copper and zinc.

aluminium A light metallic element, resistant to corrosion and a good conductor of heat and electricity. It is much used in alloys where lightness and strength are required, as in aircraft and overhead power cables.

amalgam An alloy of mercury with another metal.

ammonia A colourless pungent gas, which dissolves in water very easily. Ammonia is used in refrigerator cooling systems and to make fertilizers.

aperture Of a lens, the size of the lens opening. In a camera, the larger the aperture the more light is able to reach the film. Wide apertures are used in poor light conditions.

arc welding The fusing together of pieces of metal by using the heat produced between electrodes. *See* ELECTRODES.

asbestos A fibrous compound, mostly of magnesium and silicon, found in certain minerals. A good insulator against heat and electricity, it has been widely used in fire-proofing. It has been found, however, that its fibres can cause damage to the lungs when inhaled.

atom The smallest bit of an element that can take part in a chemical reaction or which has the properties of that element. Atoms each consist of a central core, the *nucleus*, made up of tiny particles called *protons* and *neutrons*, except in the case of hydrogen, which has no neutrons. Around the nucleus are orbiting particles called *electrons*. *See* ELECTRON; NEUTRON; PROTON.

B

battery Two or more electric cells joined together, as in a car battery. Also used incorrectly for some dry cells that are only single cells.

boiling point The temperature at which a liquid changes into a gas—that is, the temperature at which it boils.

brass An alloy of copper and zinc. The amounts of each metal can vary greatly between different brasses. Yellow brass, for example, is 67% copper, 33% zinc.

bronze An alloy mainly of copper, with a few per cent of another metal, usually tin, also zinc, manganese, aluminium, or phosphorus.

C

calcium A soft, silvery-white metal found widely in nature in combination with other elements. Limestone, for instance, is calcium carbonate.

calorie The amount of heat required to raise the temperature of 1 gram of water by 1 degree centigrade. The large calorie, written with a capital C as Calorie, is 1,000 calories. It is used as a measure of the energy value of foods.

carat A unit providing a measure of the purity of gold alloys. One carat means that there is 1 part of gold in 24 parts of alloy. Pure gold is 24 carat. Another unit called a carat is used as a standard of weight (205 mg) for precious stones.

carbon A non-metallic element found widely in nature in combination with other elements, and pure as diamonds and graphite. It occurs in all living things. *See* ORGANIC CHEMISTRY.

carbon dioxide A colourless, dense gas present in small quantities in the atmosphere and dissolved in water.

carbon monoxide A colourless, very poisonous gas formed when fuels are incompletely burnt, as in car exhaust fumes. Carbon monoxide is used in industry, and is a part of such gas mixtures as producer gas and water gas.

catalyst A substance that can speed up or slow down a chemical reaction without itself being changed at the end of the reaction. Many industrial processes, such as petroleum refining, use catalysts, which are often finely divided metals (nickel and platinum, for example) or metal oxides.

Celsius *See* CENTIGRADE.

centigrade scale A temperature scale in which the melting point of ice is taken as 0°C and the boiling point of water 100°C, at normal atmospheric pressure. It is also known as *Celsius*.

centre of gravity The point at which the weight of an object seems to be concentrated, however the body is arranged.

combustion Burning. The combination of a burning substance with oxygen in the air. Heat, light, and flame are produced.

compound A substance consisting of two or more elements combined in fixed proportions by weight. Carbon dioxide, for example, contains carbon and oxygen.

conductor A material through which heat or electricity will flow. Copper is a good conductor of both.

convection The transfer of heat in liquids and gases by movements of the molecules. Eventually, heat is distributed evenly throughout the gas or liquid.

converging lens A lens that is fatter in the middle than at the edge—a *convex* lens—and which is able to focus light rays. A magnifying glass is an example. *See also* DIVERGING LENS.

Copernicus (Niklas Koppernigk) (1473–1543) A famous Polish astronomer who first proposed that all the planets, including the Earth, revolved round the Sun.

copper A reddish-brown metal which, after silver, is the best conductor of electricity and an excellent conductor of heat. It is easily shaped, and widely used in electrical equipment and alloys such as brass and bronze.

corrosion Action on the surface of materials due to air, moisture, or chemicals. The rusting of iron or wearing away of stonework in cities are examples.

cosmic rays High-energy radiation reaching the Earth from outer space and consisting mainly of positively charged particles (protons), but also electrons and other sub-atomic particles. *See* ELECTRONS; PROTONS.

Curie A famous family of French scientists, the most noted of whom were Pierre (1859–1906) and his wife Marie (1867–1934). Pierre studied crystals with his brother Jacques, and discovered that, when certain crystals are squeezed, opposite electric charges are produced on opposing faces of the crystal. Later, with Marie, he discovered radium, and with Henri Becquerel shared the Nobel prize for physics. Marie later also won the Nobel prize for chemistry.

D

Dalton, John (1766–1844) A British scientist famous for his theories on the structure of atoms, and for his law on pressures in gases.

degree A unit of temperature. Also, a 1/360th part of a circle.

density The mass of a particular volume of a substance, usually given as the mass in grams of one cubic centimetre. It is expressed as mass/volume. *Relative density* is the density of a substance compared with that of water.

diamond A form of carbon found in the ground as crystals. It is the hardest substance occurring in nature.

diverging lens A lens that is thinner in the middle than at the edge; it is *concave*. It spreads out light rays passing through it. *See also* CONVERGING LENS.

dry cell A type of electric cell in which the electrolyte is a paste and the negative electrode is the metal can holding the paste. Dry cells are used in torches and radios.

E

Einstein, Albert (1879–1955) An American physicist (born in Germany) famous for his theory of relativity.

electric cell A device for producing an electric current by chemical action between two separate electrodes in contact with an electrolyte. Several cells together are called a battery, although torch and similar cells, which are single cells, are popularly called batteries. *See* ELECTRODE; ELECTROLYTE.

electricity *Current electricity* is a flow of electrons through substances called conductors when a circuit is completed. *Static electricity* is the build-up of charges on materials called non-conductors.

electrode Part of an electric cell through which the current enters or leaves. The positive electrode is called the *anode*, the negative electrode the *cathode*.

electrolysis The breakdown of a substance by passing an electric current through it when it is in liquid or dissolved form. Electrolysis happens in an electric cell when the electrodes are connected so that a current flows through the electrolyte. Some metals are extracted from their ores by electrolysis. Aluminium is an example.

electrolyte A substance in contact with the electrodes in an electric cell. It conducts an electric current between the electrodes. It may be a liquid, as with the acid in a car battery, or a paste, as in a dry cell. *See* DRY CELL.

electron A tiny part of an atom found outside the nucleus of that atom. Atoms of different elements have different numbers of electrons. *See* ATOM.

element The simplest form of a substance—it cannot be separated into simpler substances that still have the same properties. Gold and oxygen are examples of elements.

energy The ability or capacity for doing work. We use energy from our food when we run; a car uses the energy in petrol. There are several kinds of energy. Heat energy, light energy, and electrical energy are examples.

F

Fahrenheit A temperature scale on which the melting point of ice is taken as 32°F and the boiling point of water 212°F, at normal atmospheric pressure.

fluids Substances that flow—that is, gases and liquids. Solids cannot flow.

focal length The distance from a lens to its main focus. An example is the distance from the lens of the eye to the retina at the back. If the eye is too short or too deep for the lens to focus, then spectacles or contact lenses may be worn to correct the fault. *See* LENS.

force Anything that tends to move something that is stationary or to change the way in which a moving object moves.

freezing point The temperature at which a liquid changes into a solid.

friction A force that resists attempts to move one surface over another. Car brakes rely on the friction created between the brake surfaces.

fulcrum The point at which a lever pivots.

fuse A wire that melts if the electric current passed through it is too high.

G

Galileo (1564–1642) An Italian astronomer, physicist, and mathematician famous for his many scientific experiments. He worked on the movement of the pendulum and other moving bodies, and was the first astronomer to use a telescope, with which he discovered the mountains of the Moon. He supported Copernicus's views that the Sun is the centre of the solar system, though this brought him into serious conflict with the Church.

gas A state of matter in which the molecules can move freely. A gas has no shape. It takes the shape of the container holding it.

gears A group of wheels, usually with teeth around the edge, which move on each other and so pass on the turning movement of one shaft to another.

gravity The pull that bodies in space—the planets and the stars—exert on other bodies. The Earth's gravity, for instance, holds the Moon circling round it and traps the gases of the atmosphere. The pull of the Moon is strong enough to cause the tides on Earth.

grid system A network of power stations connected by power lines which distribute electricity from one area to another. In this way, variations in demand in local areas can be met.

H I

heat A form of energy due to the movement of molecules within a substance. The faster the molecules move, the hotter a substance is.

hologram An image of an object formed by reflected laser light. This image can be captured on a photograph. If the hologram is lit by laser light, it appears three-dimensional.

humidity The amount of water vapour present in a given volume of air.

hydraulics The use of forces in liquids. Many kinds of machinery use hydraulics. Car brakes are operated hydraulically.

ice Water in its solid form. Most solids are more dense than the liquid forms of the same substance, but ice is initially less dense than liquid water. It melts at 0°C under normal atmospheric pressure.

image The replica of an object formed by a lens or mirror through bending (refraction) or reflection of light rays.

inertia The tendency of a moving object to keep on moving or of an object that is at rest to remain still unless a force is applied to it.

insulator A substance that does not conduct heat (a thermal insulator) or electricity (an electrical insulator). Examples are plastics of various kinds.

ion An electrically charged atom or group of atoms.

isotope A different form of the same element, with a different number of neutrons in the centres of the atoms. Isotopes have similar chemical properties, but behave differently in other ways. Carbon has three isotopes, for example, with 12, 13, and 14 neutrons respectively. Carbon-12 is stable, carbon-14 radioactive.

J K

joule A unit of measurement for work and energy.

kilowatt A unit of electrical power. It equals 1,000 watts.

kinetic energy The energy of movement.

L

laser A device that produces light of high energy. A laser beam is *monochromatic* (one colour) and *coherent* (its waves are in step). The term is derived from the initial letters of 'light amplification by stimulated emission of radiation'.

Lavoisier, Antoine (1743–94) A French chemist and physicist regarded as the 'father' of modern chemistry. He explained what happens when substances burn (combustion), proving that theories then held were wrong. *See* COMBUSTION.

lens A piece of glass shaped so that it can bend light rays as required. *See* CONVERGING LENS; DIVERGING LENS.

lever A simple machine consisting of a rod or bar that pivots so that a force applied at one part can be used to move a load at another.

light A form of energy to which the eye is sensitive and representing the red to violet part of the spectrum. *See* SPECTRUM.

liquid A state of matter in which, though they move about, the molecules are kept in contact with their neighbours by forces acting between them. Liquids have no definite shape of their own.

M

machine A device that uses forces so that work can be done more easily. Levers, pulleys, gears, and wheels are examples of simple machines.

magnet A piece of metal, usually iron, that attracts other magnetic materials to it.

mass. The amount of matter that an object contains. It is not the same as weight. An object on Earth has the same mass on the Moon, but weighs only one-sixth as much as on Earth, because the force of gravity is lower on the Moon.

mechanics The study of the way in which forces act on bodies.

melting point The temperature at which a substance changes from solid to liquid.

meniscus The curved shape of the surface of a liquid due to the forces that exist between the molecules of the liquid.

metre A unit of measurement, the basic unit of the metric system. One metre equals 39·37 inches. A metre is divided into 100 centimetres and 1,000 millimetres.

mirror A highly polished surface, usually of metal, silvered glass, or plastic, that reflects light.

mixture Two or more substances mixed together, but not combined chemically. They can usually be separated by physical means—by filters or magnets, for example.

molecule The smallest portion of an element or compound that is able to exist on its own.

N

negative charge An electric charge due to the presence of electrons. *See* ELECTRON.

neutron A particle found within the atoms of elements. Hydrogen is the only element that has no neutrons in its atoms. Neutrons have no electric charge. Atoms of the same element may contain different numbers of neutrons. *See* ATOM; ISOTOPE.

Newton, Sir Isaac (1642–1727) An English physicist and mathematician who discovered many basic laws of science. His work on gravity, light, and the movement of objects makes him one of the most outstanding scientists.

nuclear reaction A reaction involving the centres or nuclei of atoms in which atoms are split with a huge release of energy. The reaction is the basis of nuclear weapons and of nuclear reactors in power stations.

nucleus *See* ATOM.

O

objective The lens of a telescope or microscope that is nearest to the object being observed.

optics The study of light.

organic chemistry The study of compounds containing carbon.

P

petroleum A certain mixture of hydrocarbons that occurs naturally. Petroleum, also known as oil, is formed over a period of millions of years from the remains of tiny plants and animals. It is refined to produce petrol (gasoline) and hundreds of other chemicals.

physics The study of energy and matter.

plastics Man-made materials that are plastic—that is, they can be moulded to shape during manufacture. There are two chief kinds: *thermosetting resins*, such as Formica, which are hard and cannot be reshaped, even by heat, once formed; and *thermoplastics*, such as polythene, which can be softened and remoulded.

polymer A chemical compound with large molecules made up of many smaller but similar molecules, rather like the links in a chain joined together. Plastics are examples.

potential energy Stored energy, as in water behind a dam.

Priestley, Joseph (1733–1804) A British scientist who did many experiments on combustion. He discovered sulphur dioxide and ammonia, and is jointly credited with the discovery of oxygen.

prism A regular block of glass—especially a triangular prism, which is able to split white light up into its colours. A prism with two sides at right-angles acts as a mirror. Such prisms are used in binoculars and periscopes.

proton An atomic particle found in the nucleus of all atoms. Each element has a characteristic number of protons. *See* ATOM.

Q R

quenching Cooling metals rapidly by immersing them in a liquid such as oil, water, or brine at room temperature to harden the metal.

radar Device used as an aid to navigation in ships and planes. It stands for 'radio direction and ranging'. Radio pulses are sent out and reflected back off objects in their path. The reflected pulses are recorded on a screen. The distance can be measured by the time taken for them to be reflected. An experienced radar operator may even be able to identify the object in the radio beam's path, such as an aircraft or ship of a particular kind.

radiation, heat One of the ways in which heat travels. It is the transfer of heat from one material to another through a medium such as air (or even through a vacuum), without the medium itself being heated.

relative density *See* DENSITY.

Rutherford, Ernest (1871–1937) British physicist famous for his work on the structure of the atom and radioactivity. He was the first person to 'split' the atom.

S

short circuit When a connection, usually accidental, is made between two wires in the same circuit, the electricity flows between them instead of following the correct path.

smelting A process for obtaining a metal from its ores. Iron and steel, for instance, are made in a blast furnace by smelting iron ore.

solid A state of matter in which the molecules attract each other strongly, so that the substance has a definite shape and size. *See* GAS; LIQUID.

solution The result when one substance dissolves in another, in the form of either a solid in a liquid or a gas in a liquid.

sonar A system for detecting objects and/or finding direction underwater. It is similar to radar, but uses very high-frequency sound waves, not radio waves. *See* RADAR.

sound A vibration picked up by the ear and identified by the brain as noise.

specific gravity Now known as *relative density*. *See* DENSITY.

spectrum (light) The range of colours obtained when white light is split up into its constituent parts. In order, they are red, orange, yellow, green, blue, indigo, and violet.

surface tension The property of a liquid that makes it behave as though the surface were covered by a skin. If a liquid is spilled on a surface, surface tension helps to restrict the flow of the liquid.

T

temperature A measure of the hotness of a body. It is measured with a thermometer on a scale in degrees. *See* CENTIGRADE; FAHRENHEIT.

tempering A process for toughening steel by reheating it and quenching it in oil or water.

thermostat A device used to regulate temperature. For instance, in a hot-water tank, when the temperature of the water reaches a preset level, the electricity supply to the immersion heater element can be cut off. It can be restored when the temperature drops again.

U V

ultrasonics The production and use of sound waves that are vibrating too quickly to be heard by the human ear.

vacuum Ideally, a space in which there are no atoms. But a perfect vacuum cannot be obtained.

vapour A substance that is in its gaseous form.

velocity The rate of movement of an object in a specific direction. It is given in distance per unit time.

volume The size of a body. In a six-sided object such as a brick, volume equals height x length x breadth.

W

weight The downward force due to gravity acting on an object. The weight of an object varies with gravity, so an object on the Moon weighs less than it does on Earth. Its mass stays the same. *See* MASS.

welding A method of joining two pieces of metal together. It involves heating the metals to be welded to high temperatures so that they fuse together. Often a welding rod is melted onto the edges of the metals being joined.

THE Body Machine

What are our bodies made of?

CELLS, LIFE'S BUILDING MATERIALS
Cells are the materials out of which all living things are made. This applies to plants just as much as to animals. A single cell is so small that it can be seen only with a microscope. The simplest plants and animals consist of only one cell. But others are made up of millions and millions of cells. Although a cell is tiny, it has a complex structure. And it lives, just as a person lives. It needs to take in oxygen, 'digests' food, and expels waste materials.

Although each person's body is made up of more than a million cells, they all developed from just two cells—the mother's egg that was fertilized by (united with) the father's sperm. All the cells are extremely tiny, but some are more than 50 times as big as others. And most of them have the same basic design. Each is enclosed in a thin skin called the *cell membrane* or *plasma membrane*. This holds the cell in shape, separates it from other cells, and protects it. Within the membrane is a watery jelly called *cytoplasm*. Many small structures live in it. Each of them has a job to do—producing energy, enabling the cell to reproduce, or breaking the cell up when it dies. Near the centre of the cell is the nucleus, the cell's control centre.

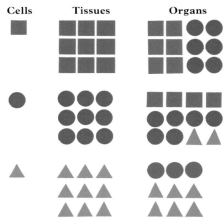

Cells   Tissues   Organs

Cells have many functions. Some manufacture chemicals that the body need. Others transport nourishment or prote the body against disease, germs, or dir Altogether, the body's cells have thousand of different jobs to do. Cells of variou kinds join with each other to form th many *tissues* in the body—such as bon muscle, or nerve. The tissues, in turn, joi together to form *organs*—such as th heart, the lungs, or the liver. Some cel live only a few days. Then they break u and are replaced by new cells. Other cel live for years. Some of the cells that mak up the nerves continue to exist for th body's whole life.

Who discovered about cells?

Robert Hooke drew the structure of a piece of cork.

Theodor Schwann drew plant and animal cells in the 1830s.

In the 1600s, an English scientist, Robert Hooke, studied a slice of cork through his home-made microscope. He saw that it had a honeycomb structure, and called the little boxes in it *cells*. In the 1830s, two German scientists, Matthias Schleiden and Theodor Schwann, helped to convince other scientists that all living things are made up of cells.

Are all cells the same?

Nerve cell

Muscle cell

Red blood cell

Brain cell

Skin cell

Cells not only differ in size and function, but each type of cell looks quite different from every other type of cell. Some are like little round blobs of jelly. Others are like tiny coils, doughnuts, needles, boxes, leaves, or space satellites. Some have no particular shape at all. But most of them have basically the same structure.

Cell membrane,
the cell's skin

Centriole,
plays a part in
cell reproduction

TYPICAL CELL

Cytoplasm,
a watery jelly that supports
the cell's structures

Mitochondrion, one of the cell's energy producers

Lysosome, one of the cell's policemen

Nucleus, the cell's brain

Why is the nucleus important?

The nucleus contains an important structure called a *nucleolus*—or several such structures. A nucleolus consists of proteins and RNA (ribonucleic acid), which plays a part in building up proteins.

Nucleus

The nucleus is a round body near the centre of the cell. It is the cell's 'brain', and controls all its activities. In it are tiny threads called *chromosomes* that carry *genes*. The genes are the cell's built-in, inherited instructions. They shape the body and everything in it, and say how all the different parts of the body will work.

How are worn-out cells replaced?

MITOSIS

1 *2* *3* *4*

A cell's chromosomes and centrioles duplicate, and begin to move to opposite sides of the cell.

The chromosomes form a 'spindle' across the cell and move to the ends. Daughter cells form.

Each minute, millions of cells in the body die and are replaced by millions of new cells. Most cells are produced by *mitosis*. This is a process in which a cell divides to form two 'daughter' cells—each exactly the same—which then develop into full, independent cells.

How many bones are there in a skeleton?

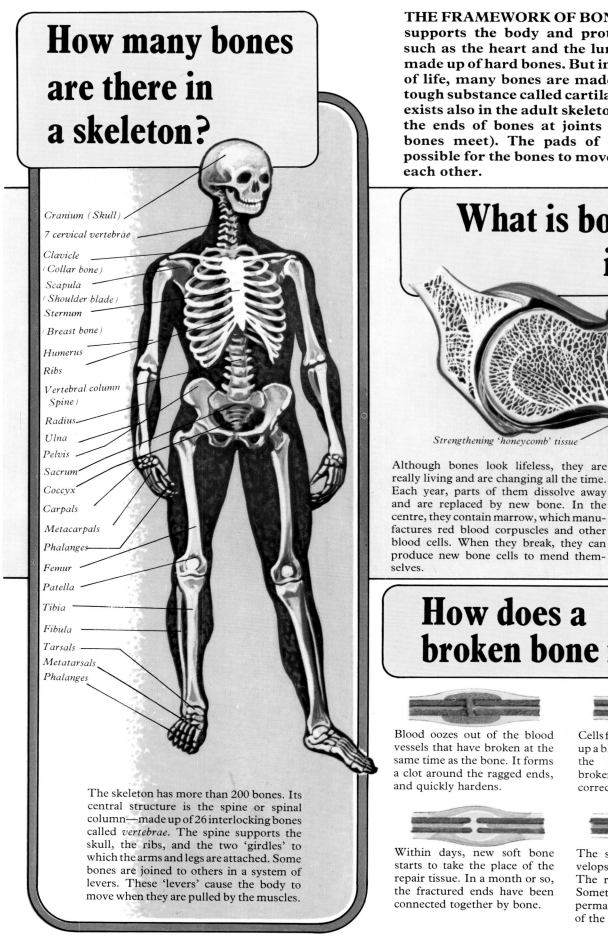

Cranium (Skull)
7 cervical vertebrae
Clavicle (Collar bone)
Scapula (Shoulder blade)
Sternum (Breast bone)
Humerus
Ribs
Vertebral column (Spine)
Radius
Ulna
Pelvis
Sacrum
Coccyx
Carpals
Metacarpals
Phalanges
Femur
Patella
Tibia
Fibula
Tarsals
Metatarsals
Phalanges

The skeleton has more than 200 bones. Its central structure is the spine or spinal column—made up of 26 interlocking bones called *vertebrae*. The spine supports the skull, the ribs, and the two 'girdles' to which the arms and legs are attached. Some bones are joined to others in a system of levers. These 'levers' cause the body to move when they are pulled by the muscles.

THE FRAMEWORK OF BONES The skeleton supports the body and protects vital organs, such as the heart and the lungs. In adults, it is made up of hard bones. But in the earliest stages of life, many bones are made of a rubbery but tough substance called cartilage. This substance exists also in the adult skeleton as pads covering the ends of bones at joints (the places where bones meet). The pads of cartilage make it possible for the bones to move smoothly against each other.

What is bone like inside?

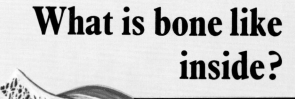

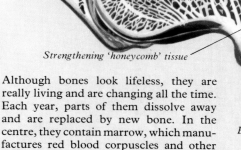

Layers of cal
phosphate a
other mat

Strengthening 'honeycomb' tissue

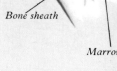

Bone sheath

Marrow

Although bones look lifeless, they are really living and are changing all the time. Each year, parts of them dissolve away and are replaced by new bone. In the centre, they contain marrow, which manufactures red blood corpuscles and other blood cells. When they break, they can produce new bone cells to mend themselves.

How does a broken bone mend?

Blood oozes out of the blood vessels that have broken at the same time as the bone. It forms a clot around the ragged ends, and quickly hardens.

Cells from the bone sheath build up a blob of repair tissue around the fracture (break). The broken ends must be held in the correct position by a splint.

Within days, new soft bone starts to take the place of the repair tissue. In a month or so, the fractured ends have been connected together by bone.

The soft bone gradually develops into strong hard bone. The repair is then complete. Sometimes, the bone remains permanently bumpy at the site of the fracture.

How do joints work?

Ball-and-socket joint at the hip allows movement in almost any direction.

Pivot joint at the elbow allows rotating movement and hinge movement.

Hinge joint at the knee allows backward and forward movement.

The body has several kinds of movable joints. Hinge joints, such as the knee joint, allow a straight backward-and-forward movement. Ball-and-socket joints, such as those at the shoulder and hip, allow movement in many directions. Pivot joints, such as the joint between the skull and the top vertebrae of the spine, allow rotating movement. The elbow is particularly flexible. It has both hinge and pivot joints.

Are there more than two bones in the skull?

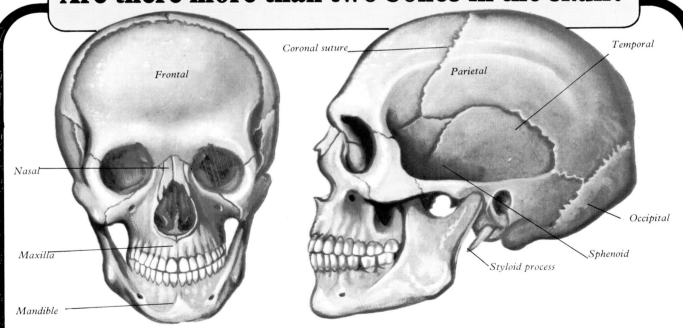

Coronal suture

Frontal

Temporal

Parietal

Nasal

Occipital

Maxilla

Sphenoid

Mandible

Styloid process

THE BONES OF THE SKULL

The skull is made up of 22 bones. Eight of them are closely interlocked, and form the cranium—the box that holds and protects the brain. The other 14 bones are known as the *facial bones*. They form the face and jaw. The only part of the skull that moves is the mandible, the lower jaw.

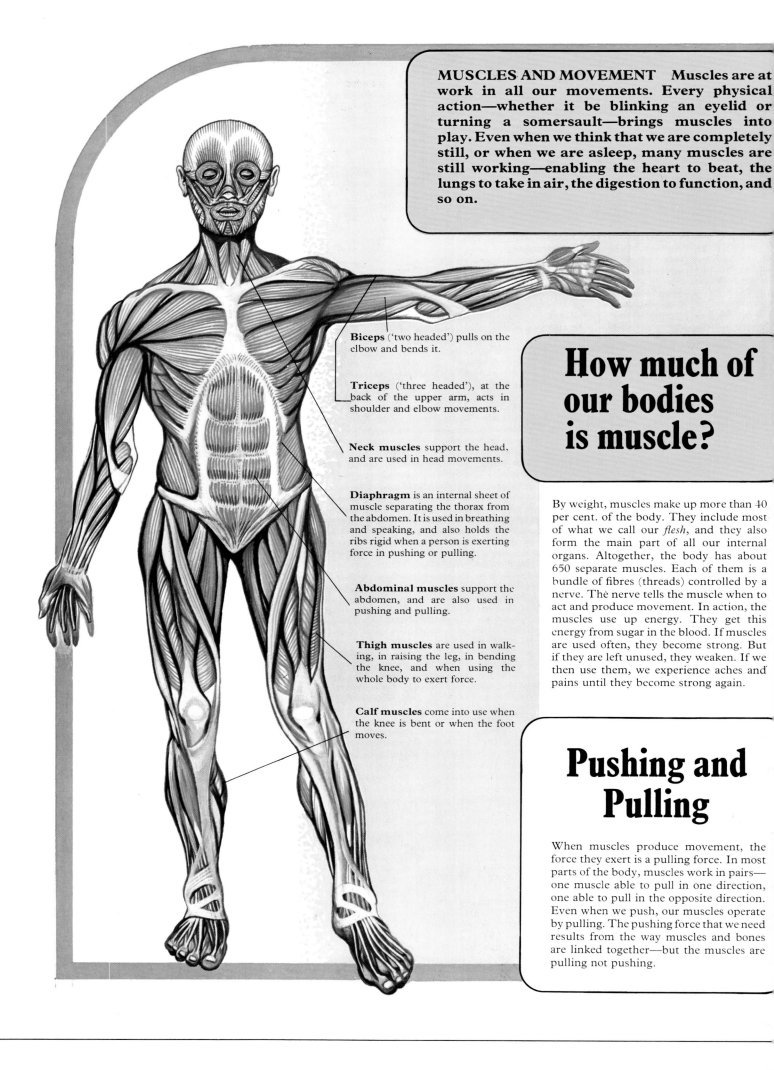

MUSCLES AND MOVEMENT Muscles are at work in all our movements. Every physical action—whether it be blinking an eyelid or turning a somersault—brings muscles into play. Even when we think that we are completely still, or when we are asleep, many muscles are still working—enabling the heart to beat, the lungs to take in air, the digestion to function, and so on.

Biceps ('two headed') pulls on the elbow and bends it.

Triceps ('three headed'), at the back of the upper arm, acts in shoulder and elbow movements.

Neck muscles support the head, and are used in head movements.

Diaphragm is an internal sheet of muscle separating the thorax from the abdomen. It is used in breathing and speaking, and also holds the ribs rigid when a person is exerting force in pushing or pulling.

Abdominal muscles support the abdomen, and are also used in pushing and pulling.

Thigh muscles are used in walking, in raising the leg, in bending the knee, and when using the whole body to exert force.

Calf muscles come into use when the knee is bent or when the foot moves.

How much of our bodies is muscle?

By weight, muscles make up more than 40 per cent. of the body. They include most of what we call our *flesh*, and they also form the main part of all our internal organs. Altogether, the body has about 650 separate muscles. Each of them is a bundle of fibres (threads) controlled by a nerve. The nerve tells the muscle when to act and produce movement. In action, the muscles use up energy. They get this energy from sugar in the blood. If muscles are used often, they become strong. But if they are left unused, they weaken. If we then use them, we experience aches and pains until they become strong again.

Pushing and Pulling

When muscles produce movement, the force they exert is a pulling force. In most parts of the body, muscles work in pairs—one muscle able to pull in one direction, one able to pull in the opposite direction. Even when we push, our muscles operate by pulling. The pushing force that we need results from the way muscles and bones are linked together—but the muscles are pulling not pushing.

How many kinds of muscle are there?

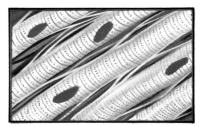

Voluntary muscle is made up of bundles of fibres. Because of their markings, they are called *striated* (striped).

There are two main kinds of muscles, voluntary and involuntary. *Voluntary* muscles are those that we can deliberately use. Examples are the muscles that come into use when we walk or talk. *Involuntary* muscles are those over which we have no control. They do their work without any knowledge or intention on our part. Examples are those that are continuously at work as the lungs breathe in and breathe out air. The heart muscles are unusual. They look like voluntary muscles, but act as involuntary muscles.

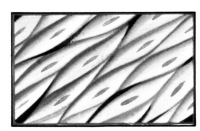

Involuntary muscle consists not of fibres but of pointed cells. It is said to be *smooth* or *unstriated* (unstriped).

How does a muscle work?

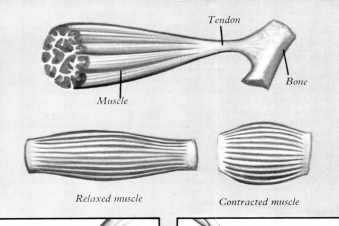

Tendon

Bone

Muscle

Relaxed muscle

Contracted muscle

Muscle relaxed

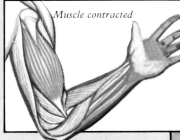

Muscle contracted

Muscles are attached to the bones of the skeleton by cords called *tendons*. If you want to lift your arms, your brain sends a signal to your arm muscles through nerves. The muscles contract (get smaller) and pull the bones of the forearm up.

Why do muscles get tired?

When a muscle works, it uses up energy. This energy comes from chemical action between glucose (stored in the muscle) and oxygen from the blood. The chemical action forms lactic acid. As the acid builds up, the muscle begins to feel 'tired'. When the muscle rests, the acid is reconverted to glucose.

How thick is our skin?

Hair

Papillae

Dead cells

Nerves

Sebaceous gland

Hair root

Hair follicle

Sweat gland

Blood vessels

EPIDERMIS

DERMIS

ADIPOSE TISSUE

The skin that we see is the *epidermis*, the skin's outer layer. Beneath it, is the thicker *dermis*, up to 3 mm (0·125 inch) in depth. The outer layer of the epidermis consists of dead cells. These gradually flake off and are replaced. The epidermis has no blood vessels, and few nerves. The dermis has both nerves and blood vessels. It also has sweat glands leading to openings (pores) on the skin surface. Hair roots are located in the dermis.

BLOOD VESSELS LOSE HEAT

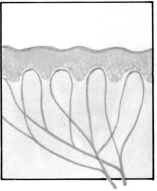

When the blood is cool, the skin's blood vessels become narrow and keep blood from the surface.

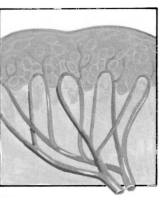

When the blood is hot, the blood vessels expand and carry it to the surface to cool.

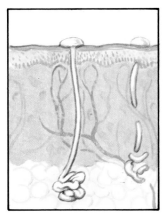

SWEAT GLAND

Sweat glands get rid of waste products and help to regulate heat.

What use is it?

The skin is waterproof. It is tough compared with many other bodily tissues, and protects the body from injury and infection. The *adipose* (fatty) tissue beneath the dermis cushions and insulates the body. Some 2 million sweat glands in the skin help to get rid of waste liquids. They also help to control the body's temperature. When we become overheated, they release water (sweat) on the skin's surface. As the water evaporates, the skin is cooled. Blood vessels in the skin also help to regulate temperature. Sebaceous (oil) glands lubricate the skin and prevent it drying out. Another important function of the skin is to protect us from harmful rays in sunlight.

Why do people have skins of different colours?

Skin colour comes from the red haemoglobin in the blood, and the brown pigment *melanin*. This pigment is produced by cells called *melanocytes* in the lower layer of the epidermis. It protects the body from harmful ultra-violet rays in sunlight. Because of the amount of protective melanin present, the peoples of hot countries have darker skins than those from cool countries.

Some peoples have little melanin. But in sunlight they 'tan'.

Other peoples have small granules of melanin in their skin.

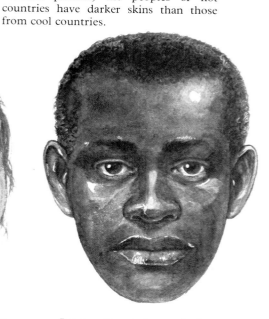

Peoples of tropical countries have much protective melanin.

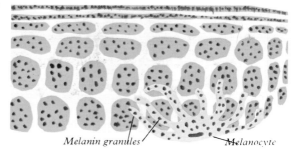

Melanin granules   *Melanocyte*

How do fingerprints help to identify people?

A fingerprint is unlike all other fingerprints, and never changes.

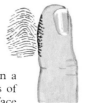

The patterns of ridges and grooves on a person's fingertips follow the patterns of *papillae* ('pimples') on the outer surface of the dermis. These patterns are called *fingerprints*. The patterns never change, even if the outer skin is damaged. And no two persons have the same patterns. For this reason, fingerprints are used by police and others as a way of identifying people.

What is hair?

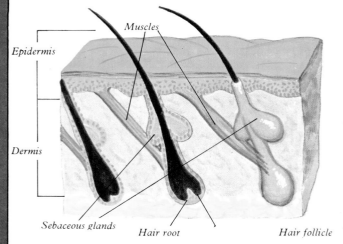

Epidermis   *Muscles*

Dermis

Sebaceous glands   *Hair root*   *Hair follicle*

Compared with other mammals, human beings have little hair. The thick hair that covers most mammals protects them and keeps them warm. It cushions the skin against injury. And in cold weather, muscles in the skin make it stand up. The erect hairs trap an insulating layer of air against the skin. Hairs grow by forming new cells at the base of the root.

Why do we have blood?

Blood has two main parts. One is a yellowish liquid called *plasma*. The other is a solid part made up of various types of cells and chemicals floating in the plasma. The chief cells are the red and white corpuscles. Red corpuscles carry oxygen to the body's tissues, and remove carbon dioxide. They contain a red substance called *haemoglobin*. White corpuscles fight germs. They include granulocytes, lymphocytes, and monocytes.

BLOOD, THE VITAL FLUID Without blood, the cells that make up the body's tissues could not live. Blood carries food and oxygen to them to nourish them and to enable new cells to develop. It also removes carbon dioxide and other waste products. It carries them away so that they can be expelled harmlessly from the body. Blood also carries hormones—the chemical substances that control many of the body's activities. Its other functions include fighting infection, and helping to control temperature by carrying excess heat to the skin surface.

Wall of blood vessel

Granulocyte

Platelet

Plasma

Cholesterol and other chemicals

Red blood cell

Monocyte

Lymphocyte

How much blood have we?

The Vital Fluid

An adult has roughly enough blood to fill seven wine bottles. More than half is plasma.

The amount of blood we have varies according to age and weight. But an adult has about 5 litres (9 pints). Blood cells wear out after a certain length of time, and have to be replaced. Each day, about one-hundredth of the blood in a person's body is used up. To replace worn-out red corpuscles, the body has to make about 115 million cells every minute. These cells are made in the bone marrow, the soft tissue inside bones.

How does blood fight germs?

When germs enter the body, millions of white blood cells leave the blood stream and enter the infected tissue to attack and digest them. In this struggle, dead germs and cells are seen as *pus*. Some strongly-resistant germs are made harmless by means of chemicals called *antibodies*. These antibodies are carried by the lymphocytes.

3. It digests the germ or kills it with chemicals.

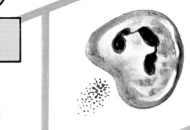

4. It expels the remains of the germ as pus.

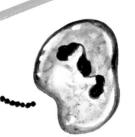

2. It spreads round the germ and 'eats' it.

1. A white blood cell moves towards a germ to attack it.

What is a blood transfusion?

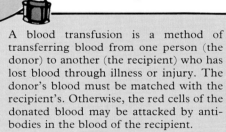

Donating blood

Receiving blood

A blood transfusion is a method of transferring blood from one person (the donor) to another (the recipient) who has lost blood through illness or injury. The donor's blood must be matched with the recipient's. Otherwise, the red cells of the donated blood may be attacked by antibodies in the blood of the recipient.

Have we all got the same kind of blood?

Group A Blood
Contains A and anti-B

Group AB Blood
Contains A and B

Group O Blood
Contains B and anti-A

Group B Blood
Contains anti-A and anti-B

Every person belongs to one of four blood groups—A, B, AB, or O. These groups are based on the presence or absence of substances called *antigens* (*A* and *B*) and *antibodies* (*anti-A* and *anti-B*). Antigen *A* and antibody *anti-A* react together and cause dangerous clotting. The same is true of *B* and *anti-B*.

Blood groups on the left are those from which blood can be received.

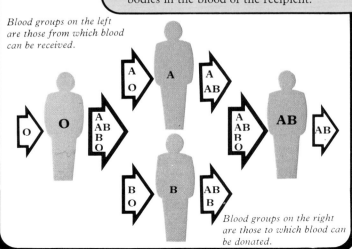

Blood groups on the right are those to which blood can be donated.

How does blood travel through the body?

BLOOD CIRCULATION AND THE HEART
Blood circulates to all parts of the body through a complicated network of blood vessels. The blood vessels in each person's body measure many thousands of miles. At the centre of the blood system is the heart—pumping tirelessly every moment of the day and night.

How does blood reach the body cells?

The arterioles and venules are linked, *below*, by tiny blood vessels called *capillaries*. In the capillaries, the rich blood from the arterioles exchanges its food and oxygen for waste materials from the body tissues. The blood then flows into the venules and back to the heart.

Temporal vein
Temporal artery
Jugular vein
Carotid artery
Subclavian artery
Subclavian vein
Pulmonary arteries
(to lungs)
Hepatic artery
(to liver)
Mesenteric artery
(to intestines)
Superior vena cava
Aorta
Pulmonary vein
Heart
Inferior vena cava
Gastric artery
(to stomach)
Renal arteries
(to kidneys)
Iliac arteries
Iliac veins
Femoral artery
Femoral vein

Capillaries
Artery
Venules
Arterioles
Vein

CAPILLARY

Blood cells pass through a capillary one at a time

Arteries (red) carry blood rich in food and oxygen from the heart to the organs and limbs. They divide into smaller vessels called *arterioles*. Veins (blue) carry blood back to the heart. The smaller veins are called *venules*.

A capillary, *above*, is so small that it can be seen only under a microscope. Food and oxygen from the rich arterial blood pass through its thin walls into the body's cells. In return, carbon dioxide and other waste materials enter the capillary, and are carried away by the blood.

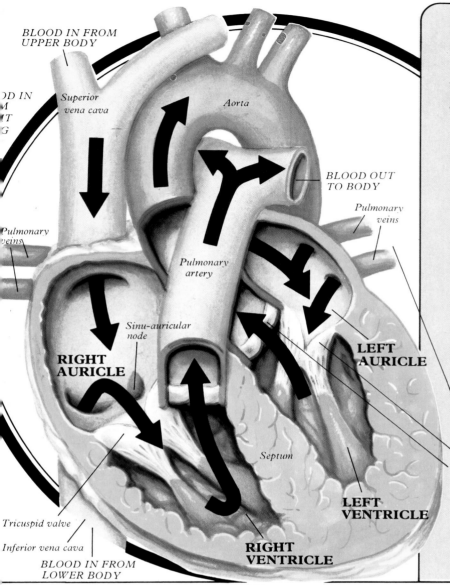

BLOOD IN FROM
UPPER BODY

OD IN
M
T
G

Superior
vena cava

Aorta

BLOOD OUT
TO BODY

Pulmonary
veins

Pulmonary
veins

Pulmonary
artery

Sinu-auricular
node

**RIGHT
AURICLE**

**LEFT
AURICLE**

BLOOD IN FROM
LEFT LUNG

Mitral valve

Semilunar valve

Septum

**LEFT
VENTRICLE**

Tricuspid valve

Inferior vena cava

BLOOD IN FROM
LOWER BODY

**RIGHT
VENTRICLE**

What does the heart look like?

The heart is a strong muscular organ enclosed in a protective bag called the *pericardium.* It pumps blood around the body under pressure. Its pumping action is the beating that we feel. It beats about 70 times a minute. Large veins bring blood to the heart. Arteries carry blood from the heart to all parts of the body. Inside, the heart is divided into two by the *septum,* a wall of muscle running down the centre. On each side of the septum there are two chambers, one above the other. The upper chambers are called *auricles,* the lower chambers *ventricles.* The left auricle collects oxygen-carrying blood from the lungs. The right auricle collects 'stale' blood from the veins. The left ventricle pumps the oxygen-carrying blood out to the body's cells. The right ventricle pumps the 'stale' blood to the lungs to be renewed.

How does it work?

Valves control the flow of blood through the heart by opening and shutting at the correct times. They are called the *mitral, tricuspid,* and *semilunar* valves.

The heart muscles pump by alternately contracting (shrinking) and relaxing. The *sinu-auricular node* in the right auricle acts as the heart's pacemaker.

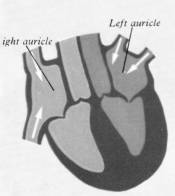

right auricle

Left auricle

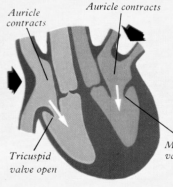

Auricle
contracts

Auricle contracts

Tricuspid
valve open

Mitral
valve open

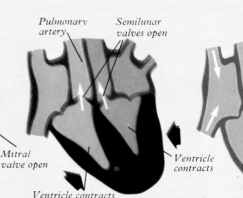

Pulmonary
artery

Semilunar
valves open

Aorta

Ventricle
contracts

Ventricle contracts

Blood flows into the left and right auricles. Then the mitral and tricuspid valves open.

The auricle muscles contract and push the blood through the valves into the ventricles.

The ventricles contract and push the blood through the semilunar valves out into the arteries.

The semilunar valves close. Blood flows into the auricles for the next heartbeat.

Why do we need to breathe?

THE BREATH OF LIFE Day and night throughout our lives, our lungs perform their rhythmic work, breathing in and breathing out air. We have no control over this process. We can hold our breath for a short while, but we soon have to give up, and then our lungs start their work again. Breathing, or external respiration, is the taking-in of oxygen and the giving-off of carbon dioxide. It is one of the basic processes of life, and nearly all living things have to breathe in order to live.

Red blood cells carry oxygen to the tissues, then return to the lungs for more.

The body's millions of cells obtain energy from food. The food releases energy when it combines with oxygen from the air we breathe.

Are our lungs hollow?

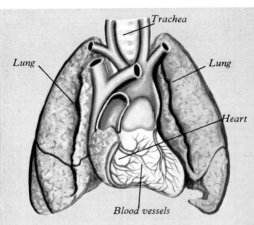

Trachea

Lung

Lung

Heart

Blood vessels

Our lungs are suspended in the *thorax* (chest cavity), one on each side of the body. They consist of soft, spongy tissue made up of millions of tiny air *sacs* (bags). When we breathe in, our lungs fill with air, rather like sponges soaking up water.

What happens when we breathe?

Breathing consists of two processes, *inspiration* (breathing in) and *expiration* (breathing out). During inspiration, the ribs are lifted outwards, and the diaphragm—the muscular wall at the bottom of the chest cavity—contracts (gets smaller). As a result, the chest cavity becomes bigger, and the lungs expand to fill it. As they do so, they draw air in through the nose and down the *trachea* (windpipe). The air enters the lungs through the bronchial tubes, and passes through a network of smaller tubes into tiny air sacs called *alveoli*. There, oxygen from the air enters the bloodstream. Carbon dioxide leaves the bloodstream, and enters the alveoli. It is then breathed out by the lungs in the process of expiration.

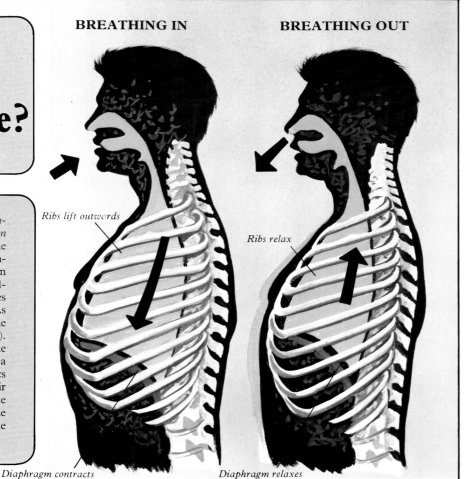

BREATHING IN

Ribs lift outwards

Diaphragm contracts

BREATHING OUT

Ribs relax

Diaphragm relaxes

How does the blood exchange oxygen for unwanted gases?

Each alveolus is inside a 'string bag' of capillaries—tiny blood vessels. The wall between the air in the alveolus and the blood in a capillary is so thin that gases can freely pass through it. Blood entering the capillaries is short of oxygen. While circulating through the body, it has given away all its oxygen to the body's cells. It is also carrying the waste gas carbon dioxide. The red corpuscles in the blood pick up oxygen from the air in the alveolus, and carry it away to the cells that need it. At the same time, the carbon dioxide seeps into the alveolus, and is expelled from the body when air is breathed out.

Oxygen-rich blood leaves the lungs

Artery

ALVEOLUS

Carbon dioxide

Oxygen

Vein

Oxygen-starved blood enters the lungs

Oxygen   *Red corpuscles*

Air in lung

Carbon dioxide

In the lungs, blood loses carbon dioxide and gains oxygen.

Muscle   *Oxygen*

Red corpuscles

Carbon dioxide

In the tissues, blood releases oxygen. It absorbs carbon dioxide.

Where does food go when we eat?

EATING AND DRINKING The cells that mak[e] up the various parts of the body must have [a] constant supply of food if they are to remai[n] healthy and do their job. By the process o[f] digestion, the food we eat is broken down int[o] simple substances. These substances are carrie[d] round the body in the bloodstream to nouris[h] the cells. Digestion takes place in the alimentar[y] canal, which is made up of several organs, eac[h] with a particular function.

The alimentary canal is a winding t[ube] that begins at the mouth and ends at [the] rectum. In an adult, it is about 9 met[res] (30 feet) long. The food we eat pas[ses] slowly through the canal, pushed al[ong] by movements of the muscles in the ca[nal] walls. The valuable part of the food g[oes] into the blood, and the waste is expel[led] from the body.

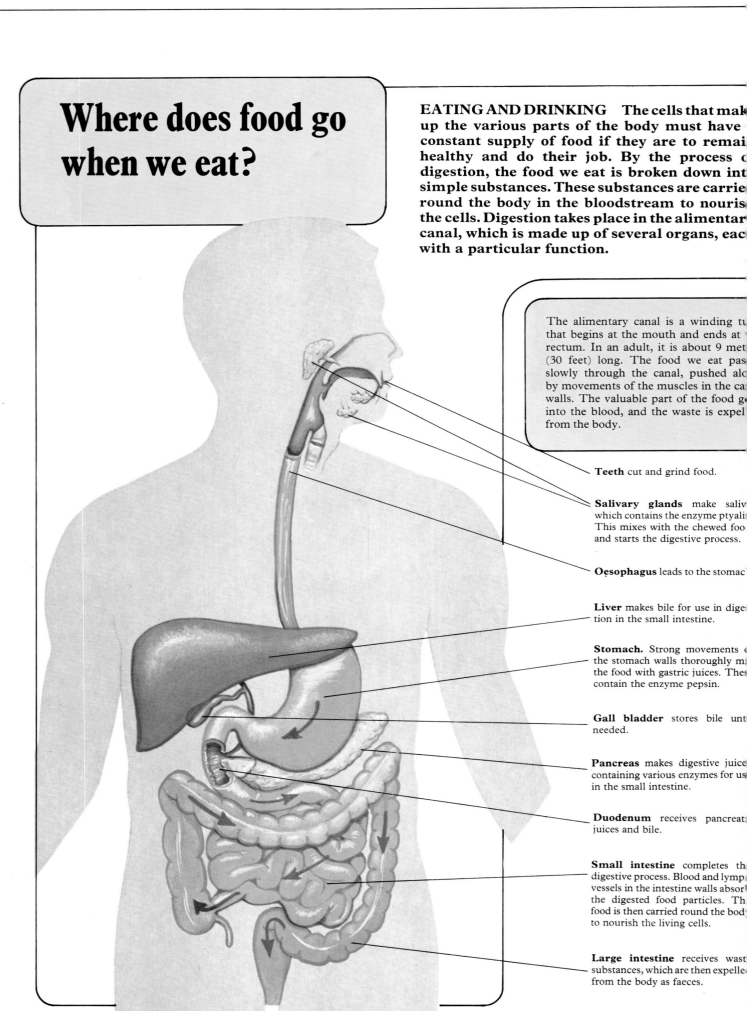

Teeth cut and grind food.

Salivary glands make saliv[a] which contains the enzyme ptyali[n]. This mixes with the chewed foo[d] and starts the digestive process.

Oesophagus leads to the stomac[h]

Liver makes bile for use in dige[s]-tion in the small intestine.

Stomach. Strong movements o[f] the stomach walls thoroughly m[ix] the food with gastric juices. The[se] contain the enzyme pepsin.

Gall bladder stores bile unt[il] needed.

Pancreas makes digestive juice[s] containing various enzymes for us[e] in the small intestine.

Duodenum receives pancreat[ic] juices and bile.

Small intestine completes th[e] digestive process. Blood and lymp[h] vessels in the intestine walls absor[b] the digested food particles. Th[e] food is then carried round the bod[y] to nourish the living cells.

Large intestine receives wast[e] substances, which are then expelle[d] from the body as faeces.

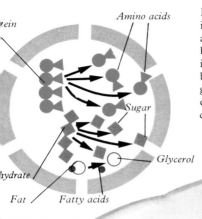

Amino acids

Sugar

Glycerol

Fat *Fatty acids*

ein

ydrate

During digestion, food is broken down into substances that the blood can carry and the cells can absorb. Carbohydrates become sugars, and proteins are turned into amino acids. Some fats pass into the blood, others become fatty acids and glycerol, and pass into the lymph. Body chemicals called *enzymes* help these digestive changes.

How is it broken down in the body?

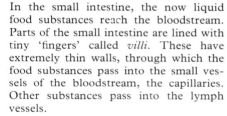

Villi

SMALL INTESTINE

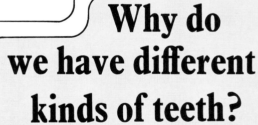

Blood capillaries

Villi

How does digested food leave the small intestine?

In the small intestine, the now liquid food substances reach the bloodstream. Parts of the small intestine are lined with tiny 'fingers' called *villi*. These have extremely thin walls, through which the food substances pass into the small vessels of the bloodstream, the capillaries. Other substances pass into the lymph vessels.

Why is the liver important?

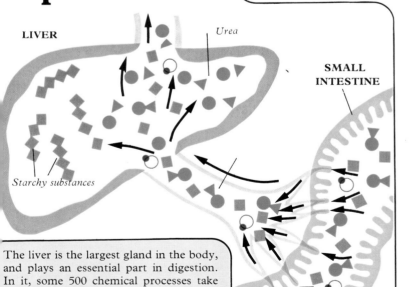

LIVER

Urea

Starchy substances

SMALL INTESTINE

The liver is the largest gland in the body, and plays an essential part in digestion. In it, some 500 chemical processes take place. Through the hepatic portal vein, it receives most of the food substances from digestion. It stores some, and regulates the amount of food that enters the main part of the body's bloodstream.

Why do we have different kinds of teeth?

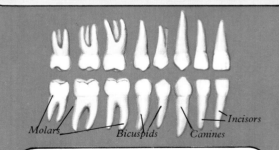

Molars *Bicuspids* *Canines* *Incisors*

Chewing is the first process in digestion. Our teeth are designed to cut, tear, and grind food. The incisors bite or cut food into pieces. The canines tear it into smaller pieces. The bicuspids crush hard lumps, and the molars, at the back, grind the food to pulp.

Why do we have glands?

GLANDS AND HORMONES The body has several control systems. Each takes part in regulating the development and working of the body's organs, in warning against danger, and in protecting the body from injury. Our nerves make up one of the most important of these systems. Our glands make up another. The glands are like little factories, manufacturing chemicals that they release into the body. Among these chemicals are the hormones that travel round the body in the bloodstream.

Over-activity of the pituitary gland leads to excess growth.

Normal activity of the gland results in 'normal' growth.

In general, the glands control the body's day-to-day functioning. They affect its shape, its strength, its reproduction, its growth, and its nourishment. A hormone from the pituitary gland causes us—most of us—to grow to about 'average' height. Other glands enable us to digest our food. Without them, not even a feast would tempt us to eat.

Under-activity of the gland results in too little growth.

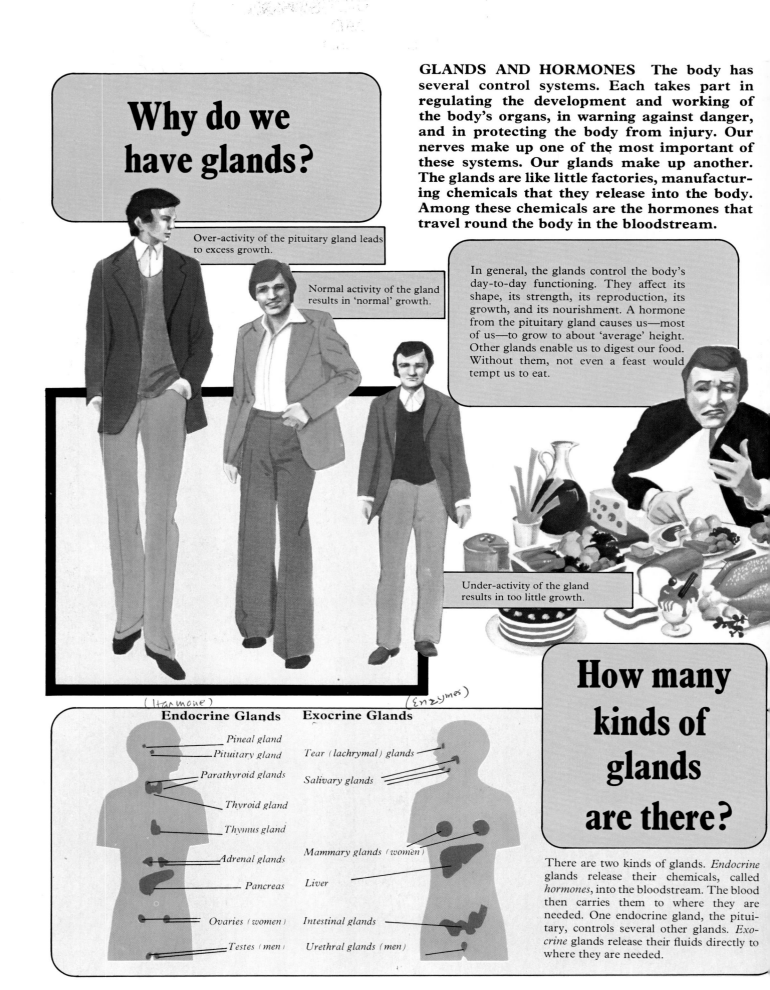

(Harmone)

(Enzymes)

Endocrine Glands

- Pineal gland
- Pituitary gland
- Parathyroid glands
- Thyroid gland
- Thymus gland
- Adrenal glands
- Pancreas
- Ovaries (women)
- Testes (men)

Exocrine Glands

- Tear (lachrymal) glands
- Salivary glands
- Mammary glands (women)
- Liver
- Intestinal glands
- Urethral glands (men)

How many kinds of glands are there?

There are two kinds of glands. *Endocrine* glands release their chemicals, called *hormones*, into the bloodstream. The blood then carries them to where they are needed. One endocrine gland, the pituitary, controls several other glands. *Exocrine* glands release their fluids directly to where they are needed.

What work is done by our kidneys?

Our kidneys filter out waste products from our blood. These waste materials are then expelled from the body in a fluid called *urine*. The kidneys are not the only organs employed in cleaning the body internally. The lungs, the skin, and the liver do similar work. The kidneys have another important function. They maintain the proper balance between water and salts in the body.

Renal vein
Renal artery

Kidney   **Kidney**

Ureters

Bladder

How does a kidney machine work?

People whose kidneys do not work properly can have waste products removed from their bloodstream by an artificial-kidney machine. A tube from an artery carries blood into the machine. The blood passes through another coiled tube in a bath of filtering liquid. Waste products pass from the blood into the liquid. The cleaned blood is then returned to a vein.

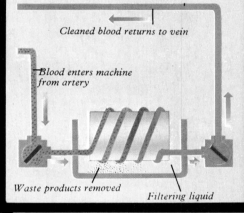

Cleaned blood returns to vein

Blood enters machine from artery

Waste products removed   *Filtering liquid*

Blood enters by renal arteries

What is a kidney like inside?

Each of us has two kidneys—one on each side—but they do not lie on the same level. The right kidney is placed lower than the left because of the position of the liver. A kidney is a brownish, bean-shaped organ. Blood vessels lead into it and from it. The blood is filtered in millions of tiny tubes coiled up in bundles called *glomeruli*.

amids of renal tubules
ect substances filtered
1 blood

Urine carried away by ureters

Filtered blood carried away by renal veins

Why do we have nerves?

Nerves are the body's 'telephone lines'. They carry information to the brain from the sense organs—the organs of sight, hearing, smell, taste, and touch. Depending on what this information is, the brain sends instructions to the muscles and glands to make the body take the appropriate action.

NERVES, A NETWORK OF COMMUNICATIONS The nervous system consists of the brain and the spinal cord, and the nerves that radiate from them. The brain and the spinal cord are together known as the central nervous system. The other nerves form the peripheral nervous system. The central nervous system works rather like an extremely complicated switchboard and computer. It receives a continuous stream of messages, and controls all the actions of the body.

Have we nerves in all parts of our bodies?

The peripheral nervous system extends into every part of the body. The nerves of the sense organs respond to their own particular stimuli (the things that rouse them to action). The eyes respond to light waves, the ears to sound waves, and so on. Other nerves, in the skin and elsewhere, respond to heat, cold, and pressure. If the stimuli are too strong, the nerves signal a sensation of pain. This is a warning to us that something is wrong.

Above: The nerves of the hand. Among the tiny organs sending them information are touch receptors—more than 1,000 in each fingertip.

Left: Nerves extend to all parts of the body. Their cells may be *sensory* (receiving information from sense organs) or *motor* (instructing muscles and glands) or both.

Are our heart-beats controlled by nerves?

The beating of the heart is controlled by a system of nerves called the *autonomic nervous system*. This system works automatically, without our being aware of it or having any control over it. It regulates all the internal organs. Its nerve cell bodies are grouped together in bundles called *ganglia*. The largest ganglion is the *solar plexus*, behind the stomach.

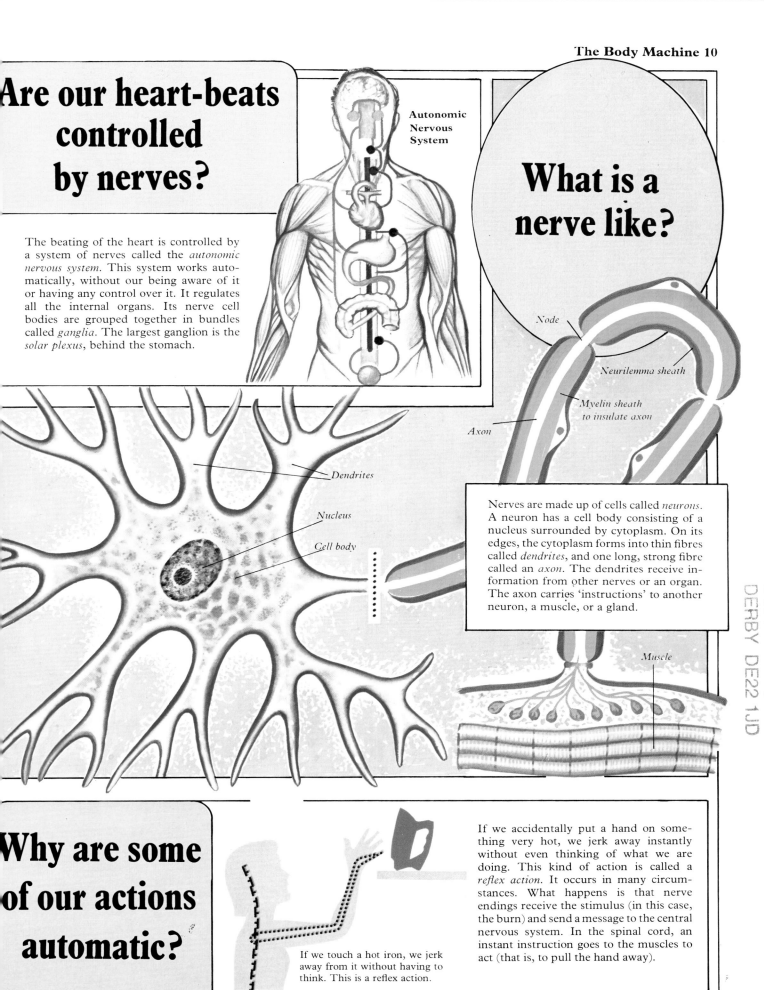

Autonomic Nervous System

What is a nerve like?

Node

Neurilemma sheath

Myelin sheath to insulate axon

Axon

Dendrites

Nucleus

Cell body

Nerves are made up of cells called *neurons*. A neuron has a cell body consisting of a nucleus surrounded by cytoplasm. On its edges, the cytoplasm forms into thin fibres called *dendrites*, and one long, strong fibre called an *axon*. The dendrites receive information from other nerves or an organ. The axon carries 'instructions' to another neuron, a muscle, or a gland.

Muscle

Why are some of our actions automatic?

If we touch a hot iron, we jerk away from it without having to think. This is a reflex action.

If we accidentally put a hand on something very hot, we jerk away instantly without even thinking of what we are doing. This kind of action is called a *reflex action*. It occurs in many circumstances. What happens is that nerve endings receive the stimulus (in this case, the burn) and send a message to the central nervous system. In the spinal cord, an instant instruction goes to the muscles to act (that is, to pull the hand away).

What does the brain do?

THE BRAIN, THE CONTROL CENTRE The brain is the organ that controls all the other organs of the body. Nothing that happens in the body can take place without the brain being involved. It is infinitely more complicated than any computer or other man-made piece of machinery. As well as being a controlling organ, it is the centre of all our thoughts and feelings. The arts and sciences of civilization all had their origins in people's brains.

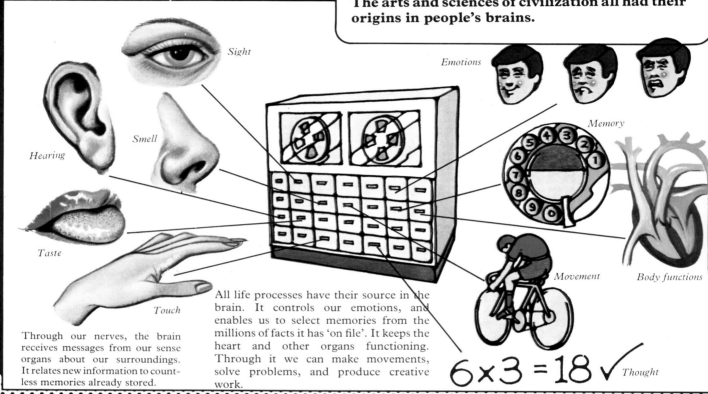

Sight *Emotions* *Memory* *Hearing* *Smell* *Taste* *Touch* *Movement* *Body functions* *Thought*

$$6 \times 3 = 18 \checkmark$$

Through our nerves, the brain receives messages from our sense organs about our surroundings. It relates new information to countless memories already stored.

All life processes have their source in the brain. It controls our emotions, and enables us to select memories from the millions of facts it has 'on file'. It keeps the heart and other organs functioning. Through it we can make movements, solve problems, and produce creative work.

What is it like?

The brain is a soft pinky-greyish mass, shaped like a large walnut. Its surface has a jumbled-up pattern of ridges and hollows, rather like that of a lump of toothpaste squeezed from a tube. It consists mainly of millions of nerve cells, called *neurons*, and supporting cells called *glial cells*. Each of the neurons is made up of a cell body and fibres that connect with other cell bodies or organs. A single neuron may be connected to hundreds of others. At one end there are several fine fibres, called *dendrites*. These receive signals from other neurons. At the other end, there is a single fibre called the *axon*. The neuron sends out its own signals over the axon. The axon fibres are called *white matter*. The rest of the cell *grey matter*.

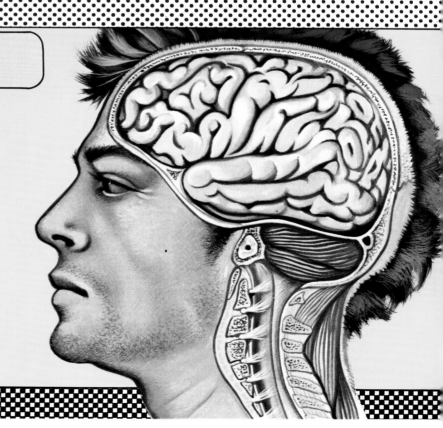

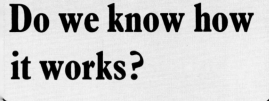

Do we know how it works?

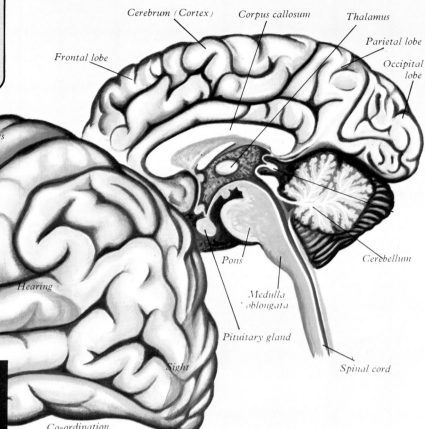

Cerebrum (Cortex)
Corpus callosum
Thalamus
Parietal lobe
Occipital lobe
Frontal lobe
Body movement
Legs
Trunk
Arms
Face
Speech
Hearing
Smell
Pons
Cerebellum
Medulla oblongata
Pituitary gland
Sight
Spinal cord
Co-ordination

Nobody really understands how the brain functions, but scientists have discovered some facts about it. It receives messages along the nerves in the form of electrical impulses. And it continuously gives off tiny electrical waves. Scientists also know that particular areas of the brain are responsible for various bodily activities.

What are our brains doing while we sleep?

During sleep, the brain is still at work. It is particularly active in the periods of sleep when the eyes make rapid movements under their lids. Perhaps it is during these periods that the brain sorts out its 'filing system'.

Have we bigger brains than other creatures?

BRAIN WEIGHTS

Whale
9 kg (20 lb)

Elephant
4·5 kg (10 lb)

Man
1·4 kg (3 lb)

Horse
0·6 kg (1·3 lb)

Eagle
0·2 kg (0·5 lb)

In the past, many people thought that human beings had bigger brains than any other creatures. In fact, many animals have bigger brains than we have. And brain weight is not related to body weight. Birds, for example, have proportionately much bigger brains than we have.

The human brain is more highly developed than the brain of any other creature. A person's intelligence or capability is not related to the size of his brain. A genius may have a smaller and lighter brain than a person of average intelligence or a feeble-minded person.

What is the inside of the eye like?

HOW WE SEE Our eyes tell us more about our surroundings than any other organ. Through them we become aware of the objects around us, and learn their size, shape, and colour. But our eyes tell us not only about objects near to us, but also about those that are a long distance away—far beyond the range of our hearing, taste, or smell. Though our eyes are the organs that collect all this information, 'seeing' takes place in our brains.

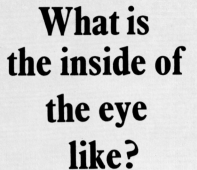

Eyelashes protect the eye from dust and dirt

Upper eyelid

Sclera

Blood vessels

Optic nerve

Vitreous humor

Cornea, the transparent front of the sclera

Pupil

Aqueous humor

Iris

Lens

Retina formed of cone and rod cells

Lower eyelid

Blind spot

The eyeball is a hollow sphere filled with watery *aqueous humor* and jelly-like *vitreous humor*. The wall of the sphere has three layers: the *retina*, the inner layer; the middle layer; and the *sclera*, the tough outer layer. The front of the sclera is transparent, and is called the *cornea*. The cornea covers the *iris* and its central hole, the *pupil*.

The retina consists of millions of light-sensitive cells, called *cones* and *rods*. The cones distinguish colours. The rods are more numerous, but build up only a black and white picture.

Rod

Cone

Does the eye work like a camera?

The eye and the camera work in similar ways. In each case, the lens focuses an inverted (upside-down) image on a light-sensitive surface. But, in the case of the eye, the image is made up of nerve impulses. These are transmitted to the brain along the optic nerve. The brain sorts out the impulses, and we see.

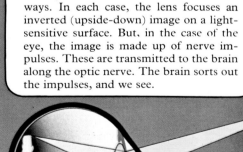

The lens focuses an image on the retina.

EYE

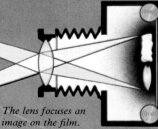

The lens focuses an image on the film.

CAMERA

In dim light, the iris opens to collect the maximum light.

Why is the pupil sometimes big and sometimes small?

The iris—the part of the eye we mean when we speak of the 'colour' of somebody's eyes—is like the diaphragm of a camera. It opens and closes to allow just the right amount of light to pass through the lens to form a clear image.

In bright light, the iris closes to cut off excess light.

Why don't we see colours in darkness?

The cones of the retina—the cells that are sensitive to colour—respond only to bright light. In daytime and under strong artificial light, they are responsible for most of our vision. But in dim light, our vision depends on the rods. These cells are very sensitive even when there is little light. But they do not detect colour, and the image they produce is not sharp. When we go from the light into the dark, the rods gradually increase in sensitivity.

Why have we two eyes?

Left eye view   **Brain combines both views**   **Right eye view**

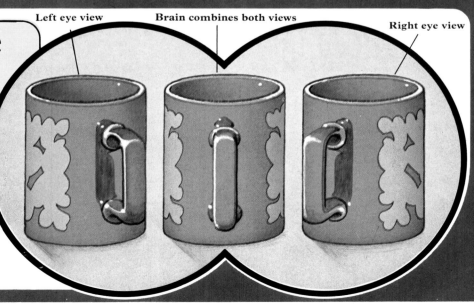

Because we have two eyes, we see an object stereoscopically—that is, in depth. Each eye forms an image of the object from a slightly different angle. The brain combines the two images to give us an impression of the object's depth. If we had only one eye, everything we looked at would seem flat.

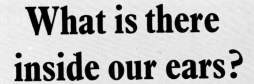

What is there inside our ears?

HEARING AND BALANCE Through our ears, we are in contact with the world of sound. Hearing is important to the body's well-being because it can often give warning of approaching danger. But it is also important to our enjoyment of life. Among our greatest pleasures are listening to the voices of those we love, to the sounds of nature, and to music and poetry. As well as being organs of hearing, our ears have another function: they help us keep our balance.

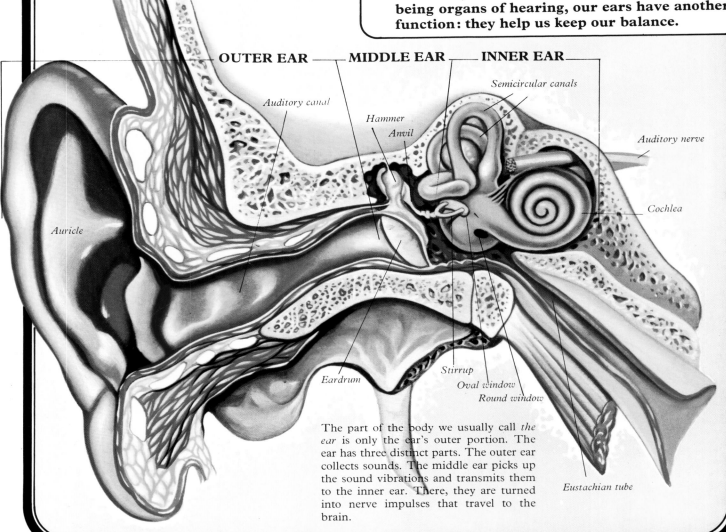

OUTER EAR — MIDDLE EAR — INNER EAR

Semicircular canals

Auditory canal

Hammer

Anvil

Auditory nerve

Cochlea

Auricle

Eardrum

Stirrup

Oval window

Round window

Eustachian tube

The part of the body we usually call *the ear* is only the ear's outer portion. The ear has three distinct parts. The outer ear collects sounds. The middle ear picks up the sound vibrations and transmits them to the inner ear. There, they are turned into nerve impulses that travel to the brain.

How do we hear?

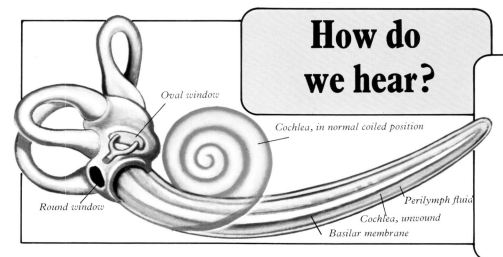

Oval window

Cochlea, in normal coiled position

Round window

Perilymph fluid

Cochlea, unwound

Basilar membrane

Sound vibrations from the *eardrum* are picked up by the *hammer*, the *anvil*, and the *stirrup*—the body's three smallest bones. The stirrup vibrates strongly against a smaller 'eardrum'—the *oval window*. These stronger vibrations cause pressure waves in the *perilymph* fluid in the *cochlea*. In turn, the pressure waves activate special sense cells, called *hair cells*, in the *basilar membrane*. These cells transmit impulses along the auditory nerve to the brain—and we hear sound.

Can we hear if our eardrums break?

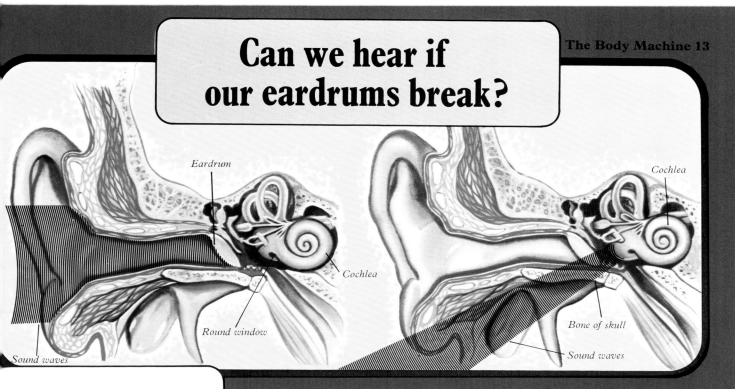

Eardrum

Cochlea

Round window

Sound waves

Cochlea

Bone of skull

Sound waves

Normally, sound picked up by the outer ear causes the eardrum to vibrate. These vibrations are transmitted to the inner ear. But if the eardrum is broken, we can still hear. Sound passes, *above*, through the hole in the drum to a smaller eardrum at the round window. This eardrum's vibrations cause pressure waves in the fluid in the cochlea. The skull bones, also, carry sound, *above right*. They transmit vibrations directly to the cochlea.

How does a deaf-aid work?

Hearing aids are used by many people who are deaf or are hard of hearing. Most aids are electronic devices, and work by transistors. Some simply make sounds louder and take them directly to the ear. Others take sounds to a bone—usually just behind the ear. The bone then transmits the sounds to the cochlea.

Why do our ears pop?

If our ears pop when we travel up or down in a lift or an aeroplane, the Eustachian tube has done its work too slowly. This tube leads from the throat to the middle ear. It lets in enough air to balance the pressures on both sides of the eardrum. But when we change height rapidly, it may not be quick enough.

How do our ears help us to keep our balance?

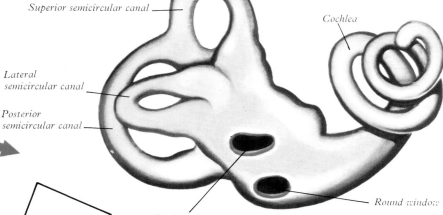

Superior semicircular canal

Lateral semicircular canal

Posterior semicircular canal

Cochlea

Oval window

Round window

If a glass of water is tilted, the water moves. The fluid in the semicircular canals moves in the same way. It tells the brain about the body's movements.

The semicircular canals of the inner ear control balance. They contain fluid that moves when we move. Nerves carry information about the fluid's movement to the brain. The brain then gives instructions to the muscles we use in keeping our balance.

What is reproduction?

REPRODUCTION—HOW LIFE CONTINUES

By the process of reproduction, a single egg cell within a woman's body develops into the millions of cells that make up a baby—a new human being. This development occurs after the egg cell has been fertilized by (united with) a sperm cell from a man. For nine months, the baby grows in its mother's womb. Then it leaves its mother's body to begin its separate existence.

Reproduction is the way in which plants and animals create more of their own kind. Some simple, one-celled animals merely split in two. This type of reproduction is called *asexual*. But in many higher forms of life, reproduction is *sexual*—a male and a female must take part in it. In human beings, a sperm cell from a man enters a woman's body and fertilizes an egg cell.

Asexual Reproduction

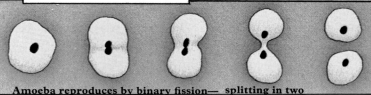

Amoeba reproduces by binary fission— splitting in two

Sexual Reproduction

Male sperm   Female egg

Which are the human reproductive organs?

Sperm cells are made in a man's testes. During intercourse, they pass through the man's penis into the woman's vagina. In one of the fallopian tubes, a sperm may unite with an egg that has developed and ripened in one of the woman's ovaries. If it does, a new life begins.

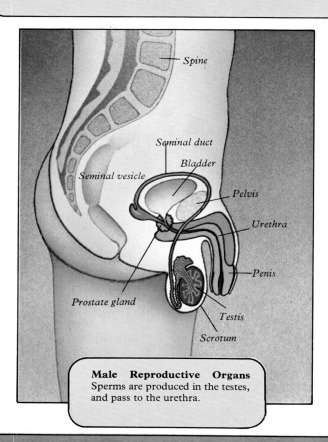

Spine
Seminal duct
Bladder
Seminal vesicle
Pelvis
Urethra
Penis
Prostate gland
Testis
Scrotum

Male Reproductive Organs
Sperms are produced in the testes, and pass to the urethra.

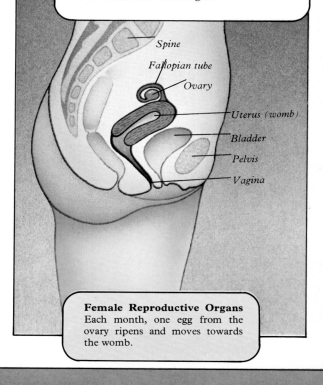

Spine
Fallopian tube
Ovary
Uterus (womb)
Bladder
Pelvis
Vagina

Female Reproductive Organs
Each month, one egg from the ovary ripens and moves towards the womb.

Fertilized egg   *Egg divides*   *Further division*   *Two weeks*   *Four weeks*   *Six weeks*   *Eight weeks*

A Foetus Grows

How does a baby grow before birth?

The egg and the sperm unite to form a cell called a *zygote*. The zygote divides into two, then these cells divide again, and so on. As the cells increase in number, they *differentiate*—that is, they form the many different kinds of cells that make up a human body. Gradually, the bundle of cells takes on human shape. In its early stages, the developing baby is called an *embryo*. At later stages, it is a *foetus*.

Do children always look like their parents?

BLUE EYES AND BROWN EYES

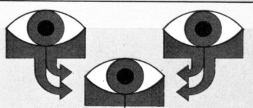

Brown-eye gene from each parent: brown-eyed child

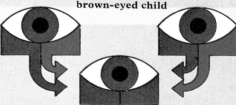

Brown-eye gene from each parent: brown-eyed child

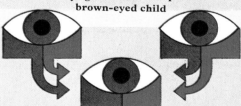

Brown-eye gene from father dominates: brown-eyed child

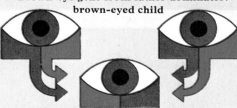

Brown-eye gene from mother dominates: brown-eyed child

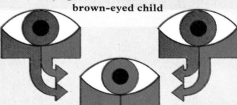

(Sometimes) Blue-eye gene from each parent: blue-eyed child

Most of the body's cells carry *genes*—the body's 'instructions' about its inherited characteristics. A child inherits some characteristics from each parent, and, as a result, is not identical with either parent.

A-Z of the Body

A

abdomen The lower part of the trunk, between the thorax and the pelvis. The diaphragm separates it from the thorax. The abdominal cavity contains the intestine, kidneys, and liver.

Achilles tendon Large tendon at the heel, extending from the calf muscles.

acupuncture A Chinese method of medical treatment by inserting needles at various points in the body.

Adam's apple The larynx. *See* LARYNX.

adenoids Glandular tissue, similar in structure to the tonsils, behind the nose. If too large, the flow of air through the nose may be obstructed.

adolescence The period during which a child's body changes into that of an adult. The change takes place between about 11 and 19 years of age.

adrenal glands Endocrine glands, one on top of each kidney. They secrete substances that control the sugar balance of the body, and that assist the body in moments of stress.

alimentary canal The long tube made up of the oesophagus, stomach, and small and large intestines. It is also called the *digestive tract*.

allergy Extreme sensitivity to substances harmless to other people. An allergy may result in a rash, asthma, or other ill effects. Milk, feathers, and dust are among the 'ordinary' substances causing allergies in some persons.

alveolus One of the tiny air spaces in the lung.

amino acid The chemical compounds from which proteins are made.

amnesia Loss of memory.

anaemia A condition in which the blood is short of haemoglobin, and consequently cannot carry enough oxygen.

anaesthetic A substance given to a patient before an operation in order to cause unconsciousness or lack of feeling.

antibiotic A substance that kills disease-producing bacteria without harming the patient. Antibiotics are produced by living organisms. A well-known one is penicillin.

antibody A substance produced by the white blood cells to combat harmful bacteria, viruses, or other organisms that have entered the body.

antiseptic A substance that kills germs.

aorta The large blood vessel that carries oxygen-rich blood from the heart to the main arteries.

appendicitis Inflammation of the appendix—the small, useless projection from the intestine.

arteriole A tiny artery.

artery One of the blood vessels (muscular tubes) carrying blood from the heart to the capillaries. The blood in all the arteries except the pulmonary artery is rich in oxygen.

artificial kidney A machine that takes the place of a missing or diseased kidney. It removes impurities from the blood.

astigmatism Defective sight resulting from the uneven curving of the eye's cornea.

B

bacterium Microscopic, single-celled organism. Some bacteria cause disease, but some help man.

bile A fluid formed in the liver and stored in the gall bladder. It aids digestion.

bladder A muscular bag that holds urine before it passes out of the body.

blood Fluid that circulates through the blood vessels. It carries oxygen and food to the tissues, and carries away waste materials. *See* RED BLOOD CELLS; WHITE BLOOD CELLS.

blood vessels The muscular tubes that carry blood through the body. They include arteries, veins, arterioles, and capillaries.

brain The body's control centre.

C

calorie Unit of heat measurement. The large Calorie equals 1,000 calories, and measures the amount of energy the body can get from food.

cancer Name given to a large number of different diseases, some of which can be cured.

capillaries Tiny blood vessels throughout the body linking the arteries to the veins. In the capillaries, oxygen is transferred to the tissues from the blood.

carbohydrates Energy-giving foods, made up of carbon, hydrogen, and oxygen. They include sugars and starches. Fats also contain carbon, hydrogen, and oxygen, though in different proportions. *See* FATS.

carbon dioxide An odourless gas produced as a waste product during respiration. We then breathe it out.

cardiac A word meaning 'concerned with the heart'.

cartilage A thick, springy substance that coats the ends of some bones at the joints. In early childhood, bones are formed from cartilage.

cell One of the minute units of which living tissue is made up.

cell division The process by which tissue is built up, each cell dividing to produce two 'daughter' cells.

chromosomes Thread-like structures in the nucleus of each cell. They carry the genes controlling the way in which the cell grows and works.

clot A thick lump of blood or other body fluid that forms when a blood vessel is cut or broken. It seals the injury and prevents blood draining away.

cochlea The inner ear to which sound travels from the ear drum.

colour blindness Inability to see the difference between various colours.

colon Part of the large intestine, adjoining the small intestine.

conception Fertilization of a female egg by a male sperm.

cone One of the light-sensitive cells in the eye's retina that reacts to colour. *See* ROD.

contagious disease One spread by close contact between people.

cornea Transparent layer of tissue covering the aperture of the eye.

corpuscle Any type of cell in the blood.

D

dandruff Inflammation of the scalp, resulting in scales being shed from the skin of the scalp.

diabetes Condition in which the level of blood sugar is too high because of shortage of the hormone insulin.

diagnosis The 'detective process' by which a doctor identifies a patient's disease.

diaphragm The muscular wall that separates the thorax from the abdomen. In breathing, it gathers together and flattens, helping to draw air into the lungs.

dietetics The study of foodstuffs and correct feeding.

digestion The process by which food is broken down into substances that can be absorbed into the blood.

digestive tract *See* ALIMENTARY CANAL.

DNA Deoxyribonucleic acid. A chemical substance of which the genes are made.

duodenum The part of the small intestine into which the contents of the stomach pass during the digestive process.

E

egg The female reproductive cell, made in the ovary.

electrocardiograph A machine used in checking the condition of the heart. It records electrical impulses from the heart muscles.

electroencephalograph A machine that records electrical impulses in the brain.

embryo A baby developing in its mother's uterus in the first weeks after the egg has been fertilized. *See* FOETUS.

endocrine gland A gland that secretes a hormone into the bloodstream to be carried to the tissues that require it. It is also called a *ductless gland*.

enzyme A chemical made in the body

that affects digestion or other bodily processes.

epidermis The outer layer of the skin.

Eustachian tube The tube that connects the middle chamber of the ear with the throat.

excretion The process by which waste materials are expelled from the body.

exocrine gland A gland that secretes substances through ducts (tubes) directly to the place where they are required by the body. Examples are the salivary and sweat glands.

F

fats Energy-giving foods made up of carbon, hydrogen, and oxygen. The body stores excess food in the form of fat.

femur The thigh bone.

fertilization The joining together of an egg and a sperm in the process of reproduction.

fever High body temperature caused by disease.

fibula *See* TIBIA.

foetus Unborn child within the uterus, at a later stage of development than an embryo.

fracture A break in a bone. In a compound fracture, the skin at the site of the fracture is also broken.

G

gall-bladder Small container beneath the liver. Bile is stored in it.

gastric A word meaning 'concerned with the stomach'.

gene Part of a chromosome responsible for the transmission of hereditary characteristics from parents to their children.

germ Word used for any organism that causes infection.

gland A collection of cells producing some substance needed by the body. *See* ENDOCRINE GLAND; EXOCRINE GLAND.

H

haemoglobin The substance in red blood cells that carries oxygen to the tissues and carries back carbon dioxide.

haemorrhage Loss of blood from a broken blood vessel, usually caused by an injury.

heart The muscular organ within the chest that acts as a pump, driving blood round the body.

hepatic A word meaning 'concerned with the liver'.

hormones Chemical substances made by the glands and carried in the bloodstream to various parts of the body. They control such body activities as growth, reproduction, and metabolism.

humerus The long bone of the arm, between the elbow and the shoulder.

hypothalamus The part of the brain that controls sleep and some other body activities.

I

ileum The part of the small intestine that connects with the colon.

infection Disease caused by bacteria, viruses, or other organisms multiplying within body tissues.

insulin A hormone secreted by the pancreas. It controls blood sugar.

intestine A long tube that forms part of the alimentary canal. It is made up of the small and large intestines.

iris The muscular diaphragm that surrounds the pupil of the eye.

JK

jejunum The section of the small intestine between the duodenum and the ileum.

joint The place where two bones meet. Some joints allow the bones to move—for example, the elbow joint. Others are fixed—for example, the pelvis.

kidneys Two bean-shaped organs in the abdomen. They rid the blood of waste products by extracting urine and other materials from it.

L

larynx The upper part of the windpipe in the throat. It contains the vocal cords. It is sometimes called the *Adam's apple.*

lens Transparent disk in the eye that focuses light rays on the retina.

ligament Tough band of tissue holding bones together at a joint.

liver Large organ within the abdominal cavity. It controls many of the body's chemical processes, and controls the amount of food in the blood. It also stores food.

lungs The two organs of respiration in the chest. In them, oxygen and carbon dioxide are exchanged between the air and the blood.

lymph Colourless fluid surrounding cells. Through it, nutrients and other materials pass between the cells and blood capillaries.

lymph system The system of tubes carrying lymph from the tissues. It empties into the blood system close to the heart.

M

mandible The lower jaw.

marrow Soft tissue in the centre of bones.

maxilla The upper jaw bones. They are fixed to the skull.

meiosis The process of cell division in which the daughter cells have only half the number of chromosomes of the parent cell.

metabolism The chemical processes by which the body builds and repairs its tissues and produces energy. The rate at which these processes take place varies according to health and other factors.

middle ear The part of the ear between the tympanic membrane and the cochlea.

mitosis The process of cell division in which the daughter cells are copies of the parent cell.

muscle A tissue that has the power to contract (shorten itself). Muscles make it possible for the body to move. They also perform many other functions, such as making the heart beat and forcing blood through the blood vessels.

N

nerve A thread-like structure composed of many nerve cells. Nerve impulses travel along the nerves between the various parts of the body.

neuron A nerve cell.

nucleus The central, controlling part of a cell. It contains the chromosomes.

O

oesophagus The gullet, the muscular tube through which food passes from the mouth to the stomach.

optic nerve The nerve that carries 'sight' from the retina of the eye to the brain.

organ A collection of cells in the body that together have a distinct shape and a special function. Examples of organs are the heart, the liver, and the lungs.

ovaries Female reproductive organs in which the ova (eggs) are developed and stored.

oxygen A gas present in air. Through the lungs, it is absorbed into the blood. It plays an essential part in metabolism.

P

palate The 'shelf' of tissue that separates the nose cavity from the mouth.

pancreas A gland in the abdomen that secretes insulin and digestive juices.

paralysis Inability to control muscular movement.

patella The knee-cap.

pelvis The 'girdle' of bone at the base of the spine. The lower limbs (the legs) are attached to it.

peristalsis Wave-like muscular movements of the walls of the intestine. The movements force food along the alimentary canal.

pharynx The throat, the cavity at the back of the mouth leading to the larynx.

pituitary gland A gland at the base of the brain. Its hormones include one that controls growth.

plasma The fluid part of blood.

proteins Substances that make up the greater part of the body. Protein foods are essential for the growth and repair of body tissues. They contain carbon, hydrogen, oxygen, and nitrogen.

puberty The stage of adolescence during which the reproductive organs and glands become mature.

pulmonary A word meaning 'concerning the lungs'.

pulse A stretching of the artery walls that takes place after each heartbeat. It can easily be felt by touching the radial artery in the wrist. A doctor counts the pulse-rate in order to check that a patient's heartbeat is normal.

pupil The aperture of the iris of the eye.

pus Thick fluid found in infected tissue. It consists of dead white cells and dead bacteria.

R

radius With the ulna, one of the bones of the forearm.

rectum The end section of the alimentary canal.

red blood cells Blood cells containing haemoglobin, by means of which oxygen is carried to the tissues and carbon dioxide carried back.

reflex action An immediate automatic response to certain kinds of stimuli. For example, a person who touches a hot surface withdraws his hand immediately without having to think about it.

renal A word meaning 'concerned with the kidneys'.

reproduction The means by which living things produce more of their own kind.

reproductive glands The organs that make reproductive cells. In men they are the testes, in women the ovaries.

respiration The process of breathing by which the body obtains oxygen from the air and gives off carbon dioxide. In the body's cells, respiration is the process by which the cells use oxygen to release energy from food.

retina The inner surface of the back of the eye, made up of cells sensitive to light. The lens of the eye throws an image on the retina of the object at which the eye is looking.

ribs The bones attached to the spinal column and enclosing the cavity in which the lungs are situated. There are 12 on each side.

rod One of the light-sensitive cells in the eye's retina. It reacts to the intensity of light, but not to colour. See CONE.

S

saliva Fluid secreted by the salivary glands. It starts the digestive process when it mixes with food in the mouth.

sperm The male reproductive cells, made in the testes.

spinal column The backbone, consisting of a column of vertebrae.

spinal cord Thick 'cord' of fibres and nerve cells running through the vertebrae of the spinal column. It forms the connexion between the brain and other parts of the body.

spleen A small organ in the abdomen, beside the stomach. It helps to filter the blood.

sternum The breastbone, joining the ribs at the front.

stimulus An occurrence that causes the body to react in some way. For example, the salivary glands react to food being put in the mouth by producing saliva.

stomach A muscular bag between the oesophagus and the duodenum which forms the first part of the alimentary canal.

sweat Fluid secreted on the skin by the sweat glands. As sweat evaporates, it helps to lower the body's temperature.

T

tendon A band of fibrous tissue joining a muscle to a bone.

testes Male reproductive organs in which sperm is developed.

thorax The chest. It contains the lungs and heart. The diaphragm separates the thorax from the abdomen.

tibia The long bone of the leg, between the knee and the ankle. The fibula lies parallel to it.

tissue A collection of similar cells with a particular function—for example, bone or muscle.

tongue Muscular organ in the mouth, used in speech, tasting, and eating.

tonsils Two glands at the back of the mouth. Their probable purpose is to defend the throat against harmful bacteria.

U

ulna With the radius, one of the bones of the forearm.

urine Fluid secreted by the kidneys. As well as water, it contains urea and other waste products.

uterus A hollow muscular organ that forms part of the female reproductive system. In it, a baby develops from embryo to foetus. It is also called the *womb*.

VW

vein One of the blood vessels (muscular tubes) carrying blood to the heart. In the pulmonary vein, between the lungs and the heart, the blood is oxygen-rich. In all other veins, the blood is dark in colour because it has lost its oxygen to the tissues and is carrying carbon dioxide.

vertebra One of the bones that make up the spinal column. A series of vertebra interlock to form the column.

viruses The smallest living organisms known, some of which cause diseases.

vitamin A chemical substance necessary for normal metabolism. Small amounts of various vitamins must be present in a person's diet.

white blood cells Cells produced in the marrow, and circulating in the blood stream. Their chief function is to fight infection.

womb See UTERUS.

STUDYING THE HUMAN BODY

The study of the human body is divided into many branches. Among the most important of them are:

Anatomy	The study of the structure of living things—not merely Man, but plants and animals of all kinds. The study of what can be seen by the eye—without the use of viewing instruments—is called *gross anatomy*. Other names are given to anatomical studies that rely on the use of microscopes. Human anatomy is concerned with all the various organs and tissues of the body. The word *anatomy* comes from Greek words meaning *to cut up*, because the earliest knowledge of anatomy was obtained by dissecting bodies.
Biochemistry	The study of the chemical substances and reactions that occur in the body. Changes in living matter, as well as the movements of living things, depend on various chemical reactions.
Cytology	The study of the structure and operation of the cells that make up the body.
Embryology	The study of the early stages in the development of living things. In the case of human beings, it relates to the stages of growth between the fertilization of the egg and the birth of a baby.
Histology	The study of the detailed structure of tissues. Histologists examine the structures that can be seen only with the aid of microscopes.
Pathology	The study of the effects of disease and other abnormal conditions on the body's organs and tissues.
Physiology	The study of the way in which living things function. The physiologist is concerned with the working of the body's various organs, and the way in which they work together.